Arithmetricks

Arithmetricks

50 Easy Ways to Add, Subtract, Multiply, and Divide Without a Calculator

EDWARD H. JULIUS

Illustrations by Dale M. Gladstone

WILEY

John Wiley & Sons, Inc.
New York • Chichester • Brisbane • Toronto • Singapore

Copyright © 1995 by Edward H. Julius
Published by John Wiley & Sons, Inc.

Illustrations © 1995 by Dale M. Gladstone

Library of Congress Cataloging-in-Publication Data:

Julius, Edward H.
    Arithmetricks : 50 easy ways to add, subtract, multiply, and
  divide without a calculator / Edward H. Julius.
        p.   cm.
      ISBN 0-471-10639-9 (pbk. : acid-free)
      1. Mental arithmetic—Juvenile literature.   [1. Mental
  arithmetic.   2. Arithmetic.]   I. Title.
    QA107.J84   1995
    513′.9—dc20   94-41836

Printed in the United States of America
10

In loving memory of my brother Ron

Contents

Division

Mental-Math Master Tricks

Addition

Division

Estimation Tricks

Tricks to Check Your Answer

Acknowledgments

It is rare that one writes a book without the help and encouragement of others. Accordingly, I would like to gratefully acknowledge my editor, Kate Bradford, for her superb job of editing the manuscript. In addition, my hat goes off to Steve Rodgers for his marvelous suggestions. Next, special thanks are due to Laurie Curtis-Abbe's pupils at Anacapa Middle School and to the children of Sierra Canyon School for their inspiration and advice. Finally, hugs and kisses go out to my daughter Marina for her brutal honesty in reviewing the manuscript; to my daughter Alex for her proficiency with the copier; and to my wife, Marion, for her constant support and love.

Arithmetricks

Introduction

Welcome to the fascinating world of arithmetricks. What are arithmetricks? They are many different ways of adding, subtracting, multiplying, and dividing faster than you ever thought possible. Most of them can be done without pencil or paper, because most of the work will be done in your head. Sometimes you'll get the answer faster than you could have with a calculator!

As a mental-math wizard, you'll be able to impress your friends and family. You'll have an advantage on math tests, and you'll learn to love working with numbers.

Now you may be wondering, "Why should I learn to do all this stuff in my head when I can just use a calculator?" Here are some typical situations in which arithmetricks can come in handy:

- When you're at the store or any place away from home or school where you don't have a calculator
- When you want to look smart. Think of how embarrassed you'd feel if you were asked to multiply 2 by 3 and had to pull out your calculator to get the answer. Now think of how proud you'd feel if you were asked to divide 32 by 5 and came up with the answer almost instantly!
- When you want to do a calculation secretly. Let's say you think a store clerk has asked you for too much money or has given you too little change in return. It will embarrass the clerk and take a lot of time if you redo the math on your calculator.
- When your calculator is broken or its batteries just died
- When you're not allowed to use a calculator, as when you're taking certain tests
- When you want the answer fast. Many calculations are actually *faster* to do in your head than on a calculator—once you know the tricks.

1

As you work your way through *Arithmetricks,* please keep the following in mind:

- You must practice, practice, practice these tricks to master them. Rapid math cannot be learned overnight. Yet, you can still have a lot of fun along the way!
- You probably have already used some math tricks without realizing it. I'll never forget the time my daughter was just learning addition, and I saw her add 8 + 7 in almost no time. When I asked her how she got the answer so quickly, she said, "Well, I know that 8 + 8 = 16, so 8 + 7 must equal one less than 16." She had just used a mental-math trick.
- The more tricks you master, the more often you'll be able to perform mental math. But don't expect to learn all the tricks in one day or even in one week. If you learn only one or two tricks per day, that will be plenty.
- Even if a trick saves only a picosecond (that's one-trillionth of a second), it's worth using. Well, maybe just half a second.
- You'll need to hide your calculator immediately! I'll pause for a moment while you do that.

To become a mental-math wizard, you don't have to be an Einstein. All you need is a basic understanding of addition, subtraction, multiplication, and division. For some of the tricks, you'll also need to know a little bit about fractions and decimals.

To get the most out of *Arithmetricks,* review the math concepts on pages 5 through 7 before you begin. They are extremely important. You can also refer to Appendix A for any symbols and terms used in this book that you don't understand. If you read something that doesn't make sense to you, ask your teacher or another grown-up for some help.

If there are some tricks you don't like (or find too difficult), don't use them. If you use only a dozen of the 50 tricks presented in this book, you'll still be in great mental-math shape.

In Appendix B, you'll find some dynamite parlor tricks that you can perform. They all take some practice, but never fail to impress, amuse, and amaze!

So fasten your seat belt, put on your thinking cap, and get ready for a journey into numbers unlike any you've ever taken.

A Note to Teachers

This book can be used to supplement a math textbook. Try going over the first 20 basic tricks with your students and have them do the practice exercises on their own. The self-teaching nature of this book will enable more able students to move on to the mental-math master tricks, estimation tricks, and checking techniques.

Arithmetricks should help many students become more enthusiastic, motivated, and confident in dealing with numbers.

Review of Some Important Math Concepts

The Concept of Place Value

It is important that you understand what each digit within a number stands for. For example, the numbers 437 and 374 contain the same three digits. But they do not represent the same amount because the digits have different "place values."

In the number 437, the "7" is the ones digit. It equals 7×1, or 7. The "3" is the tens digit. It equals 3×10, or 30. The "4" is the hundreds digit. It equals 4×100, or 400. So the number 437 can be thought of as $400 + 30 + 7$. On the other hand, the number 374 equals $300 + 70 + 4$.

Place value also applies to decimals. Let's look at the number 5.29. The "5" is the ones digit, and equals 5×1, or 5. The "2" is the tenths digit. It equals $2 \times 1/10$, or 2/10. The "9" is the hundredths digit. It equals $9 \times 1/100$, or 9/100. So the number 5.29 can be thought of as $5 + 2/10 + 9/100$. It can also be described as $5 + 29/100$.

Different Ways to Express the Same Number

There are certain ways a number can be written without changing its value. Let's take the number 58. It can be written as 58.0, 58.00, and so on, and still mean 58. It can also be written as 058, 0058, and so on, and still mean 58. (It is unusual, however, for a number such as 58 to be written as 058 or 0058.)

On the other hand, the numbers 508 and 580 would *not* mean the same as the number 58.

Numbers Can Be Added in Any Order

You can add numbers in any order to get the same sum. For example, the addition problem $32 + 19 + 66$ could be written

5

as 66 + 32 + 19 (or in four other ways) and still produce the answer, 117.

Numbers Can Be Multiplied in Any Order

You can also multiply numbers in any order to get the same product. For example, the multiplication problem 8 × 13 could be written as 13 × 8 to produce the answer, 104.

What It Means to Square a Number

When you square a number, you are multiplying the number by itself. For example, 8^2 (spoken as "eight-squared") is the same as 8 × 8, or 64.

Subtraction Is the Inverse (Opposite) of Addition

Subtraction can be thought of as the opposite of addition. For example, 14 + 7 = 21. Turning things around, you could then say that 21 − 7 = 14, and 21 − 14 = 7.

Division Is the Inverse (Opposite) of Multiplication

Division can be thought of as the opposite of multiplication. For example, 6 × 9 = 54. Turning things around, you could then say that 54 ÷ 9 = 6, and 54 ÷ 6 = 9.

Division Can Be Shown in Three Different Ways

You can show a division problem in three different ways. For example, 13 divided by 2 can be written as 13 ÷ 2, as $2\overline{)13}$, or as 13/2. In school, you probably learned that 13 ÷ 2 = 6 r 1 (6, remainder 1). However, that answer is more commonly shown as 6.5 or 6½.

How Decimals and Fractions Relate

A number might be a whole number, such as 7, 18, or 206. Or it might fall between two whole numbers, such as 81.7 or 36¾.

As just shown, both decimals and fractions are used to show part of a whole. It's important to know what they mean and how a fraction can be expressed as a decimal (or the other way around).

Page 121 of Appendix A shows some common fractions and what decimals are equivalent, or the same. For example, the fraction ¼ is equivalent to 0.25. So a number such as 13¼ could also be written as 13.25.

The Ballpark Test

Whenever you complete a calculation, you should always give your answer a quick check to see if it seems to be "in the ballpark." In other words, always check to see if your answer looks right. Let's say you've just added 93 and 98 and arrived at the answer 201. You know that each of the numbers being added is less than 100. So the sum of the two should be less than 200. Therefore, 201 is too high to be the answer. (The sum is actually 191.)

A ballpark test should also be done for multiplication, division, subtraction, and squaring. Sometimes it's difficult to apply the ballpark test, especially if the numbers involved are large. With practice, though, you'll be able to quickly spot an incorrect answer. When this happens, simply redo the calculation until it looks right.

BASIC MENTAL-MATH TRICKS

#1

Jigsaw Puzzle Fun

Adding without Carrying

Someone has given you a 500-piece jigsaw puzzle as a birthday present. During the next four days you put together 79 pieces, 48 pieces, 67 pieces, and 58 pieces. You'd like to figure out the total number of pieces you have put together. To solve this problem, you would add 79 + 48 + 67 + 58.

─────────────*Here's the Trick*─────────────

You can add these numbers *without carrying* by adding each column and then adding the totals. First add the ones column, and write down the total. Then add the tens column, and write down that total one place to the left. Finally, add the column totals, and you've got the answer. Let's try this "no-carry" method on our jigsaw puzzle example.

✎ **Problem:**   79
  79 + 48 + 67 + 58   48
                                                          67
                                                        + 58
                                                        ────
Step 1. Add the ones column ⟶   32
Step 2. Add the tens column ⟶   22
                                                        ────
                            Answer: 252 pieces

✎ Let's try another one: 73
  73 + 18 + 54 + 36   18
                                                          54
                                                        + 36
                                                        ────
Step 1. Add the ones column ⟶   21
Step 2. Add the tens column ⟶   16
                                                        ────
                            Answer: 181

FOOD FOR THOUGHT   This trick will also work when adding numbers in the hundreds. Just write the total of the hundreds column another place to the left, and then add! Now and then you will have to carry when using this trick, but not often.

―――――――――*Now It's Your Turn*―――――――――

I. 74	2. 32	3. 44	4. 15	5. 78	6. 86
22	59	14	47	91	44
36	47	83	63	25	58
+ 55	+ 60	+ 92	+ 52	+ 48	+ 92
17					
17					
187					

(*See answers on page 137.*)

#2

She Sells Seashells by the Seashore

Adding by Altering

One of your favorite activities at the beach is collecting seashells. This morning you collected 29 seashells, and this afternoon you collected 44. How many seashells did you collect altogether? To solve this problem, you would add 29 + 44.

_____*Here's the Trick*_____

Whenever you're adding a number that ends in 9, first *add* 1 to the number in your head. So a number like 29 would become 30. Then *subtract* 1 from the other number. So a number like 44 would become 43. Finally, add the two "new" numbers, and you've got the answer. Let's use this trick to see how many seashells you collected.

✎ **Problem:** 29 + 44

Step 1. Add 1 to the 29 ⟶ 29 + 1 = 30
Step 2. Subtract 1 from the 44 ⟶ 44 − 1 = 43
Step 3. Add the 43 to the 30 ⟶ 30 + 43 = 73

    Answer: 73 seashells

✎ Let's try one more example: 59 + 35

Step 1. Add 1 to the 59 ⟶ 59 + 1 = 60
Step 2. Subtract 1 from the 35 ⟶ 35 − 1 = 34
Step 3. Add the 34 to the 60 ⟶ 60 + 34 = 94

    Answer: 94

FOOD FOR THOUGHT Multiples of 10 (like 20, 30, and so on) are always easier to add than nonmultiples. This trick begins by changing the number ending in 9 to a multiple of 10. When you're adding a number that ends in 8, add 2 to change it to a multiple of 10. Then subtract 2 from the other number. Finally, add the two new numbers, and you've got the answer. So 48 + 26 becomes (48 + 2) + (26 − 2), or 50 + 24, which equals 74.

___Now It's Your Turn___

1. 49 + 25 = **74**
2. 56 + 39 =
3. 72 + 19 =

4. 89 + 44 =
5. 33 + 69 =
6. 59 + 97 =

(See answers on page 137.)

#3

Merry-Go-Round Ride

Adding Out of Order by Tens

You and your family are at a carnival, and you're about to take a ride on the merry-go-round. There are 6 horses, 4 camels, 7 giraffes, and 3 elephants. How many people are able to ride on the merry-go-round at one time? To solve this problem, you would add 6 + 4 + 7 + 3.

_____*Here's the Trick*_____

When adding, try to spot combinations of 10, even if you have to add slightly out of order. Numbers that add to 10 are the easiest and quickest to work with. All of the following pairs of digits add to 10: 1 + 9, 2 + 8, 3 + 7, 4 + 6, and 5 + 5. Let's try this trick out on our merry-go-round question.

✎ **Problem:** 6 + 4 + 7 + 3

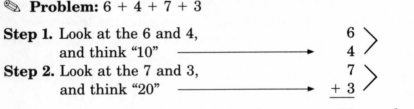

Step 1. Look at the 6 and 4, and think "10" ⟶

Step 2. Look at the 7 and 3, and think "20" ⟶

$$\begin{array}{r} 6 \\ 4 \\ 7 \\ + \ 3 \end{array}$$

Answer: 20 people

✎ Let's look at another example: 8 + 4 + 2 + 9 + 1

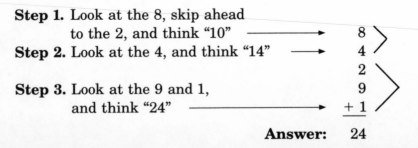

Step 1. Look at the 8, skip ahead to the 2, and think "10" ⟶

Step 2. Look at the 4, and think "14" ⟶

Step 3. Look at the 9 and 1, and think "24" ⟶

$$\begin{array}{r} 8 \\ 4 \\ 2 \\ 9 \\ + \ 1 \end{array}$$

Answer: 24

FOOD FOR THOUGHT There is often more than one way to add out of order by tens. In the example we just did, you could have noticed that 9 + 1 equals 10 right after seeing the 8 + 2 as 10. You would then think "10, 20, 24." The 4 is added last. Don't skip around too much, though, because you might forget and leave a digit out of your calculation.

—————Now It's Your Turn—————

1. 5 + 3 + 5 + 7 + 2 = **22**
2. 9 + 1 + 8 + 6 + 4 =
3. 3 + 5 + 5 + 4 + 7 =

4. 8 + 7 + 5 + 1 + 9 =
5. 2 + 4 + 4 + 6 + 3 =
6. 7 + 5 + 3 + 9 + 5 =

(See answers on page 137.)

#4

Lemonade for Sale

Subtracting by Adding—Part One

It's a hot summer day, and you and your best friend have set up a lemonade stand on your street corner. You start the day with 32 lemons. After one hour, you only have 18 lemons left. How many lemons have you used so far? To solve this problem, you would subtract 18 from 32.

_____*Here's the Trick*_____

Instead of subtracting to find the answer, try adding. It is usually easier to add than to subtract, and it's especially easy to add tens. Since subtraction is the opposite of addition, to calculate $32 - 18$, you can ask yourself, "18 plus what will equal 32?" Let's try this method on our lemonade problem.

✎ **Problem:** $32 - 18$

Step 1. Think, "18 plus what equals 32?"
Step 2. Think, "$18 + 10 = 28$" and "$28 + 4 = 32$." You have added 10 and then 4. Now add these together to get the answer.

   Answer: 14 lemons

✎ Let's look at one more example: $54 - 28$

Step 1. Think, "28 plus what equals 54?"
Step 2. Think, "$28 + 10 = 38$," "$38 + 10 = 48$," and "$48 + 6 = 54$." You have added 20 ($10 + 10$), then 6, to get the answer.

   Answer: 26

FOOD FOR THOUGHT At first, you might have to use your fingers to count the number of tens added. With practice, though, you'll be able to get the answer in one step.

Now It's Your Turn

Solve these subtraction problems by adding.

1.	23 − 7 = **16**	4.	62 − 37 =
2.	41 − 26 =	5.	50 − 11 =
3.	36 − 19 =	6.	84 − 37 =

(*See answers on page 137.*)

#5

Basketball Fever

Subtracting by Adding—Part Two

You've just been to your first professional basketball game. The home team won by the score of 111 to 85. By how many points did the home team win? To solve this problem, you would subtract 85 from 111.

_____***Here's the Trick***_____

The quick way to get the answer is to subtract by adding the difference between the two numbers and 100. For this trick, one number has to be *above* 100, and the other number has to be *below* 100. In our basketball example, 111 is above 100 and 85 is below 100. To solve the problem, ask yourself how far 111 is from 100. Then ask yourself how far 85 is from 100. Add the two amounts, and you've got the answer.

✎ **Problem:** 111 − 85

Step 1. Think, "111 is 11 above 100."
Step 2. Think, "85 is 15 below 100."
Step 3. Add: 11 + 15 = 26

   Answer: 26 points

✎ Let's look at one more example: 134 − 97

Step 1. Think, "134 is 34 above 100."
Step 2. Think, "97 is 3 below 100."
Step 3. Add: 34 + 3 = 37

   Answer: 37

FOOD FOR THOUGHT   This trick will also work when the numbers involved are on opposite sides of 200, 300, and so on.

_____*Now It's Your Turn*_____

Solve these subtraction problems by adding.

1. 107 − 92 = **15**
2. 106 − 88 =
3. 112 − 75 =

4. 121 − 93 =
5. 111 − 65 =
6. 148 − 89 =

(*See answers on page 137.*)

#6

Stuck on Stickers

Multiplying with Zeroes

One of your hobbies is collecting stickers. In all, you have 30 sheets of stickers. Each sheet has 50 stickers on it. How many stickers do you have altogether? To solve this problem, you would multiply 30 by 50.

─────────────────*Here's the Trick*─────────────────

The key is to ignore the zeroes in the ones place when starting the calculation. So to solve the sticker problem, you would multiply 3 × 5, instead of 30 × 50. You would then put the zeroes back after you have finished the multiplication. Now let's multiply 30 × 50 and see how many stickers you've collected.

✎ **Problem:** 30 × 50

Step 1. Remove the right-hand
      zeroes ⟶ 30 × 50 becomes 3 × 5
Step 2. Multiply ⟶ 3 × 5 = 15
Step 3. Put back the two zeroes
      that were removed ⟶ 15 becomes 1,500

    Answer: 1,500

✎ Now try this calculation: 70 × 400

Step 1. Remove the right-hand
      zeroes ⟶ 70 × 400 becomes 7 × 4
Step 2. Multiply ⟶ 7 × 4 = 28
Step 3. Put back the three zeroes
      that were removed ⟶ 28 becomes 28,000

    Answer: 28,000

FOOD FOR THOUGHT This trick won't work when the zeroes are in the *middle* of the number. So it won't work for 704 and 2,001. But it *will* work for 60, 900, and 1,200. Just remember to put back all the zeroes at the end.

──────────── *Now It's Your Turn* ────────────

1. 6 × 90 = **540**
2. 200 × 5 =
3. 80 × 70 =

4. 1,100 × 3 =
5. 500 × 40 =
6. 60 × 300 =

(See answers on page 137.)

#7

Candles Galore

Multiplying by 10

It's your sister's 10th birthday. As she's about to blow out the candles on her birthday cake, you think, "Wouldn't it be funny if there were one candle to blow out for each month she's been alive?" How many candles would that be? To solve this problem, you would multiply 10 by 12, since there are 12 months in a year.

_____Here's the Trick_____

This is the easiest trick of them all. To multiply a number by 10, simply place a zero at the end of the number. So to multiply 12 by 10, place a zero after the 12 to get 120. Get the idea? Now what if there were one candle for every day your sister's been alive? If we ignore the extra day for leap year, you would multiply 365 by 10. Let's try that calculation below.

✎ **Problem:** 365 × 10

Step 1. Place a zero after the 365 $\longrightarrow$ 3,650

   Answer: 3,650

What if you multiply a number with a decimal by 10? Just move the decimal point one place to the right to get your answer.

✎ Let's try 3.14 × 10.

Step 1. Move the decimal point one
   place to the right $\longrightarrow$ 3.14 becomes 31.4

   Answer: 31.4

FOOD FOR THOUGHT   What if you'd like to multiply a number by 100? Simply place two zeroes at the end of the number. So 12 × 100 equals 1,200. If you're multiplying a number with a decimal by 100, move the decimal point two places to the right. So 3.14 × 100 equals 314.

───────────────*Now It's Your Turn*───────────────

1. 27 × 10 = **270**
2. 81 × 10 =
3. 46 × 100 =

4. 3.9 × 10 =
5. 1.23 × 10 =
6. 9.87 × 100 =

(See answers on page 137.)

#8

Card Trick

Multiplying by 4

Have you ever noticed that a deck of cards is divided into four suits? The suits are spades, clubs, hearts, and diamonds. Each suit contains 13 cards—ace, two, three, and so forth. If a deck of cards contains four suits, and there are 13 cards to a suit, how many cards are there in an entire deck? (Jokers don't count.) To solve this problem, you would multiply 13 by 4.

_____*Here's the Trick*_____

To multiply a number by 4, simply double the number, then double again. Let's try this for our card problem.

✎ **Problem:** 13 × 4

Step 1. Double the 13   ⟶   13 × 2 = 26
Step 2. Double the 26   ⟶   26 × 2 = 52

    Answer: 52 cards

✎ Let's try 23 × 4

Step 1. Double the 23   ⟶   23 × 2 = 46
Step 2. Double the 46   ⟶   46 × 2 = 92

    Answer: 92

FOOD FOR THOUGHT To practice this trick, try doubling every number in sight. If you see a 36 on a street sign, double it in your head. If you see a 92 on your math test, double it, too. After a while, you'll have no problem multiplying by 4.

———————Now It's Your Turn———————

1. $15 \times 4 = $ **60**
2. $18 \times 4 = $
3. $35 \times 4 = $

4. $27 \times 4 = $
5. $33 \times 4 = $
6. $42 \times 4 = $

(See answers on page 137.)

#9

At the Movies

Multiplying by 5

One Saturday afternoon, you and thirteen of your friends decide to go to the movies. Each ticket costs $5. How much will it cost the 14 of you to get into the theater? To solve this problem, you would multiply 14 by 5.

_____*Here's the Trick*_____

The quick way to multiply a number by 5 is to first cut the number in half (divide it by 2). Then multiply by 10. That's it! Let's try this terrific trick on our movie-ticket problem.

✎ **Problem:** 14 × 5

Step 1. Cut the 14 in half (divide by 2) ➝ 14 ÷ 2 = 7
Step 2. Multiply the 7 by 10 ⟶ 7 × 10 = 70

   Answer: $70

✎ Now try this one: 22 × 5

Step 1. Cut the 22 in half (divide by 2) ➝ 22 ÷ 2 = 11
Step 2. Multiply the 11 by 10 ⟶ 11 × 10 = 110

   Answer: 110

FOOD FOR THOUGHT   This is a good trick because it is much easier to divide a number by 2 than it is to multiply it by 5. To make this trick easier, practice dividing every number in sight by 2. For example, if you see a 92 on a mailbox, cut that number in half in your head.

_____*Now It's Your Turn*_____

1. $16 \times 5 = $ **80**
2. $34 \times 5 = $
3. $26 \times 5 = $

4. $18 \times 5 = $
5. $32 \times 5 = $
6. $48 \times 5 = $

(See answers on page 138.)

#10

Up, Up, and Away!

Multiplying by 11

Eleven children are about to take a balloon ride. The balloon cannot carry more than 800 pounds. The children weigh an average of 63 pounds each. Will the balloon be able to carry the 11 children? To solve this problem, you would multiply 63 by 11 and see if this amount is greater than 800.

———————————*Here's the Trick*———————————

To multiply a two-digit number by 11, first write the two digits of the number in the answer space, but leave a space in the middle of the two digits. Then add the two digits together. Write that sum in the space you left between the original two digits. Let's try this trick out on our balloon problem.

✎ **Problem:** 63 × 11

Step 1. Write the number 63 in the answer
space, leaving a space in the
middle ——————————————➤ 6 ? 3

Step 2. Add the 6 and the 3 ——————————➤ 6 + 3 = 9

Step 3. Place the sum (9) between the 6 and
the 3 ——————————————➤ 6 9 3

Answer: 693 pounds, which is less than the 800-pound
limit

✎ Now let's try one when you have to "carry": 76 × 11

Step 1. Write the number 76 in the answer
space, leaving a space in the
middle ——————————————➤ 7 ? 6

Step 2. Add the 7 and the 6 ⟶ $7 + 6 = 13$

Step 3. Place the ones digit of the sum (3) between the 7 and the 6 ⟶ 7 3 6

Step 4. Add 1 to the hundreds digit (the 7) → 8 3 6

  Answer: 836

FOOD FOR THOUGHT In our example above (76×11), the 7 and the 6 total more than 9. Therefore, we had to "carry" by converting the 7 into an 8 in step 4.

_____*Now It's Your Turn*_____

I. $35 \times 11 = $ **385**

2. $72 \times 11 = $

3. $24 \times 11 = $

4. $16 \times 11 = $

5. $57 \times 11 = $

6. $49 \times 11 = $

(See answers on page 138.)

#11

Staying Cool at the Pool

Squaring Any Number Ending in 5

One of your favorite summer activities is to go swimming at the YMCA. The other day you beat your old record by swimming 25 laps. If each lap is 25 yards, how many yards did you swim in all? To solve this problem, you would multiply 25 by 25.

───────────────*Here's the Trick*───────────────

You can use this trick for calculations such as 55 × 55, 85 × 85, and 25 × 25 (all are squares of numbers ending in 5). To get the left-hand part of the answer, multiply the tens digit of the number being squared (2 in our pool problem) by the next whole number (or 3). The right-hand part of the answer will always be 25, so you place this next to the answer you got above. Now let's find out how many yards you've just swum.

✎ **Problem:** 25 × 25

Step 1. Multiply the tens digit   2 × 3 = 6 (left-hand
       (2) by the next whole   part of the answer)
       number (3) ──────────┘

Step 2. Put 25 after the 6 ⟶ 625

    Answer: 625 yards

✎ Let's square one more number ending in 5: 45 × 45

Step 1. Multiply the tens digit   4 × 5 = 20 (left-hand
       (4) by the next whole   part of the answer)
       number (5) ──────────┘

Step 2. Put 25 after the 20 ⟶ 2,025

    Answer: 2,025

FOOD FOR THOUGHT   The number you always use for the right-hand part of the answer (25) is easy to remember because 5×5 = 25 (and 5 is the ones digit in these calculations).

Now It's Your Turn

1.	$15 \times 15 = \mathbf{225}$	4.	$95 \times 95 =$
2.	$85 \times 85 =$	5.	$35 \times 35 =$
3.	$65 \times 65 =$	6.	$75 \times 75 =$

(See answers on page 138.)

#12

A Mountain of Cookies

Multiplying Two Numbers Whose Difference Is 2

It's raining cats and dogs outside, and you and your family decide to have some fun and bake cookies. You get carried away and bake 14 baking sheets worth. Each sheet holds 16 cookies. How many cookies have you baked altogether? To solve this problem, you would multiply 14 by 16.

——————————*Here's the Trick*——————————

You can use this trick for calculations such as 11×13, 13×15, and 24×26, where the numbers to multiply differ by 2. To get the answer, square the number in between the two numbers, then subtract 1 from the result. Let's try this method to figure out how many cookies you have baked.

✎ **Problem:** 14×16

Step 1. Figure out the number in between
14 and 16 ————————➤ 15
Step 2. Square the number 15 ————➤ $15 \times 15 = 225$
(Hint: You can use trick #11 to square the 15.)
Step 3. Subtract 1 from the 225 ————➤ $225 - 1 = 224$

Answer: 224 cookies

✎ Let's try one more: 29×31

Step 1. Figure out the number in between
29 and 31 ————————➤ 30
Step 2. Square the number 30 ————➤ $30 \times 30 = 900$
(Hint: You can use trick #6 to square the 30.)
Step 3. Subtract 1 from the 900 ————➤ $900 - 1 = 899$

Answer: 899

FOOD FOR THOUGHT   The faster you can square numbers, the easier this trick will be. Numbers ending in zero (such as 20 or 30) are easy to square—just use trick #6. In the previous trick you learned how to square numbers ending in 5. To review the squares of the numbers 1 through 15, see page 120 of Appendix A.

————————Now It's Your Turn————————

1. $11 \times 13 = $ **143**
2. $21 \times 19 = $
3. $36 \times 34 = $

4. $14 \times 12 = $
5. $24 \times 26 = $
6. $99 \times 101 = $

(See answers on page 138.)

#13

Pizza Party

Multiplying by 15

It's the last day of the school year and your class is going to have a pizza party. Fifteen pizzas have been ordered, and each pizza will be cut into 8 slices. How many slices will there be in all? To solve this problem, you would multiply 8 by 15.

_____*Here's the Trick*_____

To multiply a number by 15, first multiply the number by 10 (see trick #7). Find half of that product and add it to the original product. Let's use this trick to see how many slices of pizza there will be.

✎ **Problem:** 8 × 15

Step 1. Multiply 8 by 10 ⟶ 8 × 10 = 80
Step 2. Find half of 80 ⟶ 80 ÷ 2 = 40
Step 3. Add the 40 to the 80 ⟶ 80 + 40 = 120

   Answer: 120 slices of pizza

✎ Let's try one more: 12 × 15

Step 1. Multiply 12 by 10 ⟶ 12 × 10 = 120
Step 2. Find half of 120 ⟶ 120 ÷ 2 = 60
Step 3. Add the 60 to the 120 ⟶ 120 + 60 = 180

   Answer: 180

FOOD FOR THOUGHT   Instead of multiplying by 10 and then adding half, you can first add half, and then multiply by 10. In our pizza example, you would add 8 and half of 8 (or 4) to get 12. Then multiply 12 by 10 to get the answer, 120. Use whichever way you find easier.

Now It's Your Turn

1. $6 \times 15 = $ **90**
2. $14 \times 15 = $
3. $18 \times 15 = $

4. $26 \times 15 = $
5. $32 \times 15 = $
6. $48 \times 15 = $

(See answers on page 138.)

#14

Down on the Farm

Multiplying by Splitting

You've just spent the month of July at your uncle's farm. Your job every morning was to go into the chicken coop to take in all the eggs that had just been laid. By the end of the month, the hens had laid a total of nine dozen eggs. How many eggs are there in nine dozen? To solve this problem, you would multiply 9 by 12, since there are 12 to a dozen.

_____*Here's the Trick*_____

When one number of a multiplication pair has two digits, try splitting that larger number into two parts by dividing it by 2. Let's try this method on our egg problem.

✎ **Problem:** 9 × 12

Step 1. Split the 12 into two parts   →   12 = 6 × 2
Step 2. Restate the problem   ——→   9 × 12 = 9 × 6 × 2
Step 3. Multiply 9 × 6   ——→   54
Step 4. Multiply 54 × 2   ——→   108

   Answer: 108 eggs

✎ Let's take a look at one more example: 8 × 18

Step 1. Split the 18 into two parts   →   18 = 9 × 2
Step 2. Restate the problem   ——→   8 × 18 = 8 × 9 × 2
Step 3. Multiply 8 × 9   ——→   72
Step 4. Multiply 72 × 2   ——→   144

   Answer: 144

FOOD FOR THOUGHT   In our two examples, we cut the 12 and the 18 in half. Then to solve the problems, we had to double the 54 and the 72. So the better you are at doubling numbers, the easier this trick will be for you.

_____*Now It's Your Turn*_____

1. $8 \times 16 =$ **128**
2. $5 \times 22 =$
3. $6 \times 18 =$

4. $7 \times 14 =$
5. $9 \times 16 =$
6. $12 \times 24 =$

(See answers on page 138.)

#15

Row, Row, Row Your Boat

Multiplying by Numbers Ending in $\frac{1}{2}$

It's a beautiful day in June. You and eleven of your friends have gone down to the lake to take a boat ride. Tickets cost $4.50 each. How much did the 12 of you pay in total? To solve this problem, you would multiply 12 by $4.50 (or $4\frac{1}{2}$ dollars).

─────────────── *Here's the Trick* ───────────────

Multiplying by a number ending in $\frac{1}{2}$ (or .5) is difficult. So the trick is to double it to make it a whole number. If you double the number ending in $\frac{1}{2}$, you have to cut the other number in half to get the right answer. Let's try this neat trick on our boat ticket problem.

✎ **Problem:** $12 \times 4\frac{1}{2}$

Step 1. Double the $4\frac{1}{2}$ ⟶ $4\frac{1}{2} \times 2 = 9$
Step 2. Cut the 12 in half ⟶ $12 \div 2 = 6$
Step 3. Multiply the 9 by the 6 ⟶ $9 \times 6 = 54$

   Answer: $54

✎ Let's look at one more example: $18 \times 3\frac{1}{2}$

Step 1. Double the $3\frac{1}{2}$ ⟶ $3\frac{1}{2} \times 2 = 7$
Step 2. Cut the 18 in half ⟶ $18 \div 2 = 9$
Step 3. Multiply the 7 by the 9 ⟶ $7 \times 9 = 63$

   Answer: 63

FOOD FOR THOUGHT   Another way to end a number in $\frac{1}{2}$ is to end it in .5. So if you were to see a calculation such as 7.5×6, you could use this trick by thinking of 7.5 as $7\frac{1}{2}$.

Now It's Your Turn

1. $14 \times 1\frac{1}{2} = $ **21**
2. $9\frac{1}{2} \times 4 = $
3. $6 \times 7\frac{1}{2} = $

4. $2\frac{1}{2} \times 16 = $
5. $8 \times 6\frac{1}{2} = $
6. $5\frac{1}{2} \times 24 = $

(*See answers on page 138.*)

#16

Music Awards

Dividing with Zeroes

Tonight's the night. The music awards are on TV, but you'll have to videotape them because you won't be home. The awards last three hours, and the blank tape will record 480 minutes on slow speed. How many hours are in 480 minutes, and will that be long enough to tape the entire ceremony? To solve this problem, you would divide 480 by 60, because there are 60 minutes in an hour.

_____*Here's the Trick*_____

When dividing, you can cancel an equal number of right-hand zeroes. For example, $320 \div 80$ is equal to $32 \div 8$, which equals 4. In addition, $7,200 \div 90$ is equal to $720 \div 9$, which equals 80. Finally, $5,600 \div 800$ is equal to $56 \div 8$, which equals 7. Let's now calculate $480 \div 60$ to see if you'll have enough tape for the awards ceremony.

✎ **Problem:** $480 \div 60$

Step 1. Remove one zero from each
       number ⟶ $48 \div 6$
Step 2. Divide 48 by 6 ⟶ $48 \div 6 = 8$

    Answer: 8 hours, enough for the entire ceremony

✎ Let's try one more: $36,000 \div 400$

Step 1. Remove two zeroes from each
       number ⟶ $360 \div 4$
Step 2. Divide 360 by 4 ⟶ $360 \div 4 = 90$

    Answer: 90

FOOD FOR THOUGHT Remember that you can only cancel an equal number of right-hand zeroes. So to calculate 2,005 ÷ 703, none of the zeroes could be canceled.

_____Now It's Your Turn_____

1. 400 ÷ 80 = **5**
2. 6,300 ÷ 70 =
3. 1,200 ÷ 300 =

4. 510 ÷ 30 =
5. 8,100 ÷ 90 =
6. 42,000 ÷ 1,400 =

(See answers on page 138.)

#17

At the Arcade

Dividing by 10

You and nine of your friends have been invited to spend the afternoon at the arcade. To play the games at the arcade you will need some tokens. In all, 120 tokens are bought for the ten of you. If they are to be divided evenly, how many tokens will each of you get? To solve this problem, you would divide 120 by 10.

_____Here's the Trick_____

When a number ends in a zero, you can divide it by 10 simply by removing the zero. For example, $470 \div 10 = 47$. When the number *doesn't end* in a zero, just move the decimal point of the number one place to the left. (You can think of the decimal point of a whole number as being to the right of the ones digit.) For example, $63 \div 10$ is equal to $63. \div 10$, which equals 6.3. Now let's divide 120 by 10 to see how many tokens each of you will get.

✎ **Problem:** $120 \div 10$

Step 1. Remove the zero from the 120 $\longrightarrow$ 12

    Answer: 12 tokens

✎ Let's look at one more example: $75 \div 10$

Step 1. Move the decimal point one
       place to the left $\longrightarrow$ 7.5.

    Answer: 7.5

FOOD FOR THOUGHT What if you'd like to divide a number by 100? Simply move the number's decimal point two places to the left. So 826 ÷ 100 = 8.26. If the number you're dividing ends in two zeroes, just remove the two zeroes to get the answer. So 4,900 ÷ 100 = 49.

_____Now It's Your Turn_____

1. 46 ÷ 10 = **4.6**
2. 190 ÷ 10 =
3. 288 ÷ 10 =

4. 5,300 ÷ 10 =
5. 7,400 ÷ 100 =
6. 314 ÷ 100 =

(See answers on page 138.)

#18

Marathon Run

Dividing by 4

You just love to run and you're wondering how many miles you can run in an afternoon. So one afternoon you go to your school's track and run 56 laps. If 4 laps equal one mile, how many miles did you run? To solve this problem, you would divide 56 by 4.

_____*Here's the Trick*_____

We're going to divide by 4 in two steps. First, divide the number by 2 (cut it in half). Then divide the result by 2. Let's divide 56 by 4 and see how many miles you ran that afternoon at the track.

✎ **Problem:** 56 ÷ 4

Step 1. Cut the 56 in half ⟶ 56 ÷ 2 = 28
Step 2. Cut the 28 in half ⟶ 28 ÷ 2 = 14

   Answer: 14 miles

✎ Let's look at one more example: 72 ÷ 4

Step 1. Cut the 72 in half ⟶ 72 ÷ 2 = 36
Step 2. Cut the 36 in half ⟶ 36 ÷ 2 = 18

   Answer: 18

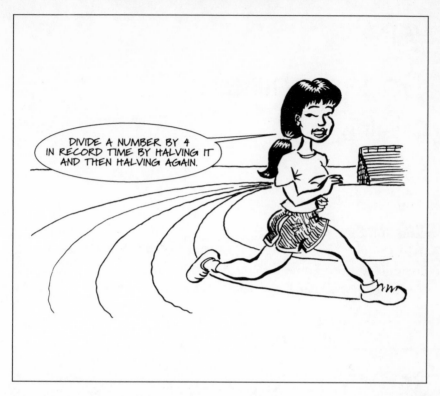

FOOD FOR THOUGHT   The faster you can divide by 2, the easier you will be able to divide by 4. The answer won't always be a whole number. For example, 50 ÷ 4 is 50 ÷ 2 = 25, 25 ÷ 2 = 12.5.

—————————*Now It's Your Turn*—————————

1. 68 ÷ 4 = **17**
2. 52 ÷ 4 =
3. 96 ÷ 4 =

4. 108 ÷ 4 =
5. 128 ÷ 4 =
6. 180 ÷ 4 =

(*See answers on page 138.*)

#19

Gone Fishing

Dividing by 5

You and four of your friends have just returned from a day of fishing. The 5 of you caught a total of 44 fish. If you've all decided to take home an equal number of fish, how many fish would that be? To solve this problem, you would divide 44 by 5.

_____*Here's the Trick*_____

The quick way to divide a number by 5 is to first multiply the number by 2 (that is, double it). Then divide the product by 10 (see trick #17). Let's solve our problem, 44 ÷ 5, and see how many fish each of you will take home.

✎ **Problem:** 44 ÷ 5

Step 1. Double the 44 ⟶ $44 \times 2 = 88$
Step 2. Divide the 88 by 10 ⟶ $88 \div 10 = 8.8$

    Answer: 8.8 (or 8⁸⁄₁₀) fish

✎ Let's "catch" another example: 73 ÷ 5

Step 1. Double the 73 ⟶ $73 \times 2 = 146$
Step 2. Divide the 146 by 10 ⟶ $146 \div 10 = 14.6$

    Answer: 14.6

FOOD FOR THOUGHT This trick relies on your ability to double numbers (to multiply them by 2). The more you practice doubling numbers, the easier this trick will be for you. So whenever you see a number (say, between 1 and 100) when you're traveling somewhere, watching TV, or doing just about anything, try doubling it!

―――――――――――_Now It's Your Turn_――――――――――

1. $32 \div 5 = $ **6.4**
2. $18 \div 5 = $
3. $27 \div 5 = $

4. $61 \div 5 = $
5. $49 \div 5 = $
6. $84 \div 5 = $

(*See answers on page 139.*)

#20

The Greatest Show on Earth

Dividing by Numbers Ending in $^1/_2$

The circus is in town. You're so excited, you'd like to invite all your friends to go with you. You've saved up $28, and tickets cost $3.50 each. How many of you can go to the circus? To solve this problem, you would divide 28 by $3.50 ($3^1/_2$ dollars).

─────────────*Here's the Trick*─────────────

Dividing by a number ending in "$^1/_2$" (or .5) is difficult. So we're going to double it to make it a whole number. But if we double the number we're dividing by, we also have to double the number we're dividing into. Let's use this trick to see how many circus tickets can be bought.

✎ **Problem:** $28 \div 3^1/_2$

Step 1. Double the $3^1/_2$ ⟶ $3^1/_2 \times 2 = 7$
Step 2. Double the 28 ⟶ $28 \times 2 = 56$
Step 3. Divide the 56 by the 7 ⟶ $56 \div 7 = 8$

Answer: 8 of you will be able to go to the circus.

✎ Let's look at another example: $33 \div 5^1/_2$

Step 1. Double the $5^1/_2$ ⟶ $5^1/_2 \times 2 = 11$
Step 2. Double the 33 ⟶ $33 \times 2 = 66$
Step 3. Divide the 66 by the 11 ⟶ $66 \div 11 = 6$

Answer: 6

FOOD FOR THOUGHT Another way to end a number in $1/2$ is to end it in .5. So if you were to see a calculation such as $26 \div 6.5$, think of the 6.5 as $6\frac{1}{2}$, and go ahead and use this trick!

_____Now It's Your Turn_____

1. $18 \div 1\frac{1}{2} = \mathbf{12}$
2. $26 \div 6\frac{1}{2} =$
3. $27 \div 4\frac{1}{2} =$

4. $20 \div 2\frac{1}{2} =$
5. $37\frac{1}{2} \div 7\frac{1}{2} =$
6. $28\frac{1}{2} \div 9\frac{1}{2} =$

(See answers on page 139.)

MENTAL-MATH
MASTER
TRICKS

#21

Gliding Across the Ice

Adding Numbers by "Seeing" Their Sum

You make a trip to the skating rink. You notice that there are 8 girls, 7 boys, 2 men, and 6 women on the ice. How many people are skating altogether? To solve this problem, you would add 8 + 7 + 2 + 6.

────────────── *Here's the Trick* ──────────────

When you add one-digit numbers, try to "see" two numbers as their sum. To add 4 + 9 + 5, many people think to themselves, "4 plus 9 equals 13, 13 plus 5 equals 18." To save time, look at the 4 and 9 and immediately think "13." Then look at the 5 and immediately think "18." So you'll look at the calculation and think "13, 18." It's as though you are "speed-reading" with numbers. Let's now try this trick on our skating problem.

✎ **Problem:** 8 + 7 + 2 + 6

    8
    7   (Don't think "8 plus 7 equals 15"; just think "15.")
    2   (Don't think "15 plus 2 equals 17"; just think "17.")
 + 6   (Don't think "17 plus 6 equals 23"; just think "23.")

Answer: 23 skaters

✎ Let's "see" another one: 5 + 7 + 4 + 9

    5
    7   (Don't think "5 plus 7 equals 12"; just think "12.")
    4   (Don't think "12 plus 4 equals 16"; just think "16.")
 + 9   (Don't think "16 plus 9 equals 25"; just think "25.")

Answer: 25

FOOD FOR THOUGHT   To force yourself to "see" two numbers as their sum (and eliminate all unnecessary thoughts), try working the following exercises *out loud*. For the first exercise, for instance, you would say aloud, "10, 19, 26."

_____*Now It's Your Turn*_____

1. 6 + 4 + 9 + 7 = **26**   4. 5 + 3 + 8 + 8 + 4 =
2. 3 + 8 + 5 + 2 =   5. 7 + 2 + 6 + 3 + 9 =
3. 1 + 6 + 9 + 8 =   6. 4 + 8 + 9 + 5 + 7 =

(*See answers on page 139.*)

#22

What's the Score?

Adding from Left to Right—Part One

You and your friend are playing your favorite word game. So far, you've scored 13, 26, 9, and 17 points. What is your score? To solve this problem, you would add 13 + 26 + 9 + 17.

─────────────── *Here's the Trick* ───────────────

One way to add a column of numbers is to add one number at a time—first the tens digit (on the left), then the ones digit (on the right). Remember that the number 26, for example, means the same as 20 + 6 (or 10 + 10 + 6). So the tens digit really means that digit times 10. Let's use this trick to see what your score is after your first four turns.

✎ **Problem:** 13 + 26 + 9 + 17

Step 1. Begin by counting "13"	13
Step 2. Add 26 (10 + 10 + 6) to 13 by counting "23,33,39"	26
Step 3. Add 9 to 39 by counting "48"	9
Step 4. Add 17 (10 + 7) to 48 by counting "58,65"	+ 17
Answer:	65 points

✎ Let's try one more addition problem: 25 + 33 + 17 + 8

Step 1. Begin by counting "25"	25
Step 2. Add 33 (10 + 10 + 10 + 3) to 25 by counting "35,45,55,58"	33
Step 3. Add 17 (10 + 7) to 58 by counting "68,75"	17
Step 4. Add 8 to 75 by counting "83"	+ 8
Answer:	83

FOOD FOR THOUGHT Trick #21 taught you to "see" the sum of two numbers. Let's look once again at the example above. When adding the 33 to the 25, don't say, "25 plus 10 equals 35, 35 plus 10 equals 45," and so on. Just say, "25, 35, 45," and so on.

_____*Now It's Your Turn*_____

1. $28 + 11 + 5 + 34 = $ **78**
2. $19 + 7 + 22 + 18 = $
3. $32 + 16 + 9 + 25 = $
4. $8 + 30 + 12 + 27 = $
5. $24 + 17 + 6 + 38 = $
6. $14 + 21 + 35 + 27 = $

(See answers on page 139.)

#23

Everybody Loves a Parade

Adding from Left to Right—Part Two

Your town always puts on a Fourth of July parade. This year's parade had four marching bands, whose members numbered 24, 15, 31, and 12. How many people in all marched in bands? To solve this problem, you would add 24 + 15 + 31 + 12.

———————————*Here's the Trick*———————————

The last trick taught you to add numbers one at a time from left to right—first the tens digit, then the ones. In *this* trick, you will learn to add all the tens digits, then all the ones digits. Remember that a number such as 24 is the same as 20 + 4. Let's use this trick to see how many people were in the parade's marching bands.

✎ **Problem:** 24 + 15 + 31 + 12

Step 1. Count all the tens digits ⟶ 20, 30, 60, 70   24

Step 2. Then add the ones digits ⟶ 74, 79, 80, 82   15

        31

     + 12

              Answer: 82 people

✎ Let's try one more addition problem:
    13 + 25 + 38 + 9

Step 1. Count all the tens digits ⟶ 10, 30, 60   13

Step 2. Then add the ones digits ⟶ 63, 68, 76, 85   25

        38

      + 9

              Answer: 85

FOOD FOR THOUGHT   Tricks #22 and #23 will also work when the numbers to add are in the hundreds, or even in the thousands. But far more concentration is needed to pull off the addition.

_____*Now It's Your Turn*_____

1. 12 + 33 + 5 + 25 = **75**
2. 24 + 7 + 16 + 32 =
3. 31 + 17 + 29 + 6 =

4. 16 + 23 + 9 + 30 =
5. 8 + 37 + 14 + 22 =
6. 20 + 18 + 34 + 4 =

(*See answers on page 139.*)

#24

A Trick for All Ages

Subtracting by Altering

Your brother and your aunt share the same birthday, May 14. The other day she turned 34, and your brother turned 9. How much older is your aunt than your brother? To solve this problem, you would subtract 9 from 34.

_____*Here's the Trick*_____

It's easiest to subtract numbers that end in zero, such as 10, 20, and 30. Whenever you are subtracting a number that ends in 9, add 1 to both numbers and you'll make the calculation much easier. Let's use this trick to see how much older your aunt is than your brother.

✎ **Problem:** 34 − 9

Step 1. Add 1 to the 34   ⟶   34 + 1 = 35
Step 2. Add 1 to the 9   ⟶   9 + 1 = 10
Step 3. Subtract 10 from 35   ⟶   35 − 10 = 25

  Answer: 25 years

✎ Let's look at one more example: 76 − 29

Step 1. Add 1 to the 76   ⟶   76 + 1 = 77
Step 2. Add 1 to the 29   ⟶   29 + 1 = 30
Step 3. Subtract 30 from 77   ⟶   77 − 30 = 47

  Answer: 47

FOOD FOR THOUGHT   This trick also works when the number you're subtracting ends in 8. In this case, you would add 2 to both numbers and then subtract. For example, 54 − 18 becomes 56 − 20 when you add 2 to each number, so it's easy to see the answer is 36.

Now It's Your Turn

1. 64 − 39 = **25**	4. 81 − 59 =
2. 72 − 29 =	5. 47 − 9 =
3. 55 − 19 =	6. 90 − 49 =

(See answers on page 139.)

#25

On the Telephone

Subtracting in Two Steps

When you picked up the telephone to call your best friend, it was 23 minutes past noon. A while later, you notice that it is 50 minutes past noon. How many minutes have you been talking on the telephone? To solve this problem, you would subtract 23 from 50.

_____*Here's the Trick*_____

The trick is to think of the second number as two numbers—the tens value and the ones value. For example, the number 16 can be thought of as 10 + 6. To subtract 16 from 30, you would first subtract 10 from 30 to get 20, then subtract 6 to get 14. Let's use this trick to solve our telephone problem.

✎ **Problem:** 50 − 23

Step 1. Show the 23 as tens and ones
values ⟶ 20 + 3
Step 2. Subtract the 20 from 50 ⟶ 50 − 20 = 30
Step 3. Now subtract the 3 ⟶ 30 − 3 = 27

  Answer: 27 minutes

✎ Let's use this trick for 120 − 76

Step 1. Show the 76 as tens and ones
values ⟶ 70 + 6
Step 2. Subtract the 70 from 120 ⟶ 120 − 70 = 50
Step 3. Now subtract the 6 ⟶ 50 − 6 = 44

  Answer: 44

FOOD FOR THOUGHT In the example above, think of the subtraction problem as 120 − 70 − 6. The first example was solved as 50 − 20 − 3.

_____*Now It's Your Turn*_____

l. 70 − 32 = **38**

2. 40 − 17 =

3. 80 − 24 =

4. 60 − 13 =

5. 110 − 48 =

6. 130 − 81 =

(See answers on page 139.)

#26
Taking a Hike
Multiplying with Decimal Points

You have just ended a three-day hiking trip. During each of the three days, you hiked 2.5 miles. (Remember that 2.5 miles is the same as 2-5/10, or 2½, miles.) How many miles did you hike altogether? To solve this problem, you would multiply 2.5 by 3.

———————————*Here's the Trick*———————————

The trick is to ignore the decimal point at the beginning of the problem, then put it back (if necessary) at the end of the problem. Let's apply this method to our hiking problem.

✎ **Problem:** 2.5 × 3

Step 1. Rewrite the problem without the
decimal point ——————————➤ 25 × 3
Step 2. Multiply ——————————➤ 25 × 3 = 75
Step 3. Put the decimal point back in
the 75 ——————————➤ 7.5

 Answer: 7.5 miles

✎ Now let's try a problem with a decimal point and zeroes:
200 × 3.3

Step 1. Rewrite the problem without the
decimal point and zeroes ——————➤ 2 × 33
Step 2. Multiply ——————————➤ 2 × 33 = 66
Step 3. Put back the two zeroes ——————➤ 6,600
Step 4: Put back the decimal point ——————➤ 660.0 or 660

 Answer: 660

FOOD FOR THOUGHT   Remember to always perform a ball-park test on your answer. In our hiking example above, you would ask yourself, "Does 7.5 *seem* to be the answer to 2.5 × 3?" That way, you'll know if you have put the decimal point back in the right place.

_____*Now It's Your Turn*_____

1. 1.2 × 3 = **3.6**	4. 3.5 × 20 =
2. 4 × 2.2 =	5. 500 × 1.1 =
3. 1.4 × 3 =	6. 7.5 × 200 =

(*See answers on page 139.*)

#27
Pedaling Power
Multiplying by 9

To prepare for the big bicycle race next month, you've been practicing every day. In fact, for the past two weeks you've cycled 9 miles per day. How many miles did you ride during that two-week period? To solve this problem, you would multiply 14 by 9 because there are 14 days in two weeks.

―――――――――*Here's the Trick*―――――――――

It's easiest to multiply by 9 in two steps. The first step is simple—multiply the number by 10. From that product, subtract the number itself and you've got the answer. Let's use this trick to see how many miles you cycled during those two weeks.

✎ **Problem:** 14 × 9

Step 1. Multiply 14 by 10 ⟶ 14 × 10 = 140
Step 2. Subtract 14 from the 140 ⟶ 140 − 14 = 126

    Answer: 126 miles

✎ Let's look at one more example: 23 × 9

Step 1. Multiply 23 by 10 ⟶ 23 × 10 = 230
Step 2. Subtract 23 from the 230 ⟶ 230 − 23 = 207

    Answer: 207

FOOD FOR THOUGHT Multiplying by 9 takes a bit more concentration than most other tricks because you have to do some subtracting in your head. (Try using trick #25 when performing the subtraction in step 2.) But with practice, you'll have this trick mastered, just like all the rest!

_____*Now It's Your Turn*_____

1. $15 \times 9 = $ **135**
2. $24 \times 9 = $
3. $13 \times 9 = $

4. $25 \times 9 = $
5. $18 \times 9 = $
6. $26 \times 9 = $

(See answers on page 139.)

#28

Selling Flowers by the Dozen

Multiplying by 12

It's Mother's Day, and the Little Shop of Flowers has sold 25 dozen roses in its first hour. How many roses has it sold so far? To solve this problem, you would multiply 25 by 12, since there are 12 to a dozen.

—————————*Here's the Trick*—————————

We are going to multiply twice and add once. First you multiply the number by 10. To that product, add twice the number. Let's now see how many roses were sold.

✎ **Problem:** 25 × 12

Step 1. Multiply 25 by 10 ⎯⎯⎯⎯▶ 25 × 10 = 250
Step 2. Multiply 25 by 2 ⎯⎯⎯⎯▶ 25 × 2 = 50
Step 3. Add the 250 and the 50 ⎯⎯⎯⎯▶ 250 + 50 = 300

    Answer: 300 roses

✎ Let's try one more: 16 × 12

Step 1. Multiply 16 by 10 ⎯⎯⎯⎯▶ 16 × 10 = 160
Step 2. Multiply 16 by 2 ⎯⎯⎯⎯▶ 16 × 2 = 32
Step 3. Add the 160 and the 32 ⎯⎯⎯⎯▶ 160 + 32 = 192

    Answer: 192

FOOD FOR THOUGHT   Like the last trick, this one takes a little more concentration. What you are doing is making your mind work like a calculator by multiplying two numbers while you remember another. It takes practice, but it's a great trick once you get the hang of it.

_____*Now It's Your Turn*_____

1. $15 \times 12 = $ **180**
2. $21 \times 12 = $
3. $18 \times 12 = $

4. $35 \times 12 = $
5. $17 \times 12 = $
6. $75 \times 12 = $

(*See answers on page 139.*)

#29

A Truckload of Crayons

Multiplying by 25

Your little sister's kindergarten class has just run out of crayons. Don't worry, though, because the school just bought 28 boxes full of crayons. If there are 25 crayons to a box, how many were bought in all? To solve this problem, you would multiply 28 by 25.

───────────────*Here's the Trick*───────────────

To multiply a number by 25, divide it by 4, and then multiply by 100. Let's try this terrific trick out on our crayon problem.

✎ **Problem:** 28 × 25

Step 1. Divide 28 by 4　　───────▶　　28 ÷ 4 = 7
Step 2. Multiply the 7 by 100　───▶　　7 × 100 = 700

   Answer: 700 crayons

✎ Let's look at one more example: 12 × 25

Step 1. Divide 12 by 4　　───────▶　　12 ÷ 4 = 3
Step 2. Multiply the 3 by 100　───▶　　3 × 100 = 300

   Answer: 300

FOOD FOR THOUGHT Sometimes the number you are dividing by 4 (in step 1) is large. In those cases, you can divide by 2, then divide by 2 again (as explained in trick #18).

Now It's Your Turn

1. $16 \times 25 = \mathbf{400}$
2. $36 \times 25 =$
3. $24 \times 25 =$

4. $44 \times 25 =$
5. $56 \times 25 =$
6. $72 \times 25 =$

(See answers on page 140.)

#30

The Undefeated Season

Squaring Any Number Ending in 1 or 9

$\mathbf{Y}$our school's volleyball team has won all 21 of its games! Let's assume it takes 21 points to win a game. How many points, in all, did your school's team score during the season? To solve this problem, you would multiply 21 by 21 (or square the number 21).

_____*Here's the Trick*_____

You can use this trick to square any number that ends in 1, like 31, 61, or 21. You can also use it to square any number that ends in 9, like 29, 99, or 49. The trick is to multiply together the two whole numbers on either side of the number you are squaring, and then add 1. Let's see how it works on our volleyball example.

✎ **Problem:** 21 × 21 (or 21²)

Step 1. Multiply the two whole numbers
on either side of 21 ————————➤ 20 × 22 = 440
Step 2. Add 1 to the 440 ————————➤ 440 + 1 = 441

    Answer: 441 points

✎ Let's look at one more example: 19 × 19 (or 19²)

Step 1. Multiply the two whole numbers
on either side of 19 ————————➤ 18 × 20 = 360
Step 2. Add 1 to the 360 ————————➤ 361

    Answer: 361

FOOD FOR THOUGHT This trick makes the calculation easier by changing one of the numbers into a multiple of 10. In our first example above, multiplying 20 by 22 was definitely easier than multiplying 21 by 21.

Now It's Your Turn

1. $11 \times 11 = $ **121**
2. $41 \times 41 = $
3. $31 \times 31 = $

4. $39 \times 39 = $
5. $29 \times 29 = $
6. $99 \times 99 = $

(*See answers on page 140.*)

#31

The Anniversary Party

Squaring Any Two-Digit Number Beginning with 5

It's your grandparents' 52nd wedding anniversary. At their party, you're thinking 52 years is a long time. Then you start to wonder how many months, weeks, and days that is. Let's just see how many *weeks* they've been married. To solve this problem, you would multiply 52 by 52 (since there are 52 weeks in a year).

───────────────*Here's the Trick*───────────────

You can use this trick to square any two-digit number that begins with 5, like 58, 55, and 52. To get the left portion of the answer, add the ones digit to the number 25. To get the right portion, square the ones digit. (Note: When squaring 1, 2, or 3, write the answer as "01," "04," or "09.") Finally, piece the two portions together. Let's now solve our anniversary problem with this trick.

✎ **Problem:** 52×52 (or 52^2)

Step 1. Add the ones digit
(2) to 25 ⟶ $25 + 2 = 27$
(left half of answer)

Step 2. Square the ones
digit (2) ⟶ $2 \times 2 = 04$
(right half of answer)

Step 3. Combine the two
halves ⟶ 2,704

Answer: 2,704 weeks

✎ Let's try one more calculation: 57×57 (or 57^2)

Step 1. Add the ones digit
(7) to 25 ⟶ $25 + 7 = 32$
(left half of answer)

Step 2. Square the ones
digit (7) ⟶ $7 \times 7 = 49$
(right half of answer)

Step 3. Combine the two
halves ⟶ 3,249

Answer: 3,249

FOOD FOR THOUGHT Notice that step 1 always involves adding the ones digit and 25. What's an easy way to remember the 25? That's right—the tens digit in all these calculations is 5, and $5 \times 5 = 25$.

—————————*Now It's Your Turn*—————————

1. $53 \times 53 = $ **2,809**
2. $58 \times 58 = $
3. $55 \times 55 = $
4. $51 \times 51 = $
5. $56 \times 56 = $
6. $59 \times 59 = $

(See answers on page 140.)

#32

The Roller-Coaster Ride

Multiplying from Left to Right

You're at the amusement park, waiting in line to ride the roller coaster. You notice that there are 13 roller-coaster cars in all. You also notice that each car holds 8 people. How many people can ride the roller coaster at one time? To solve this problem, you would multiply 13 by 8.

—————Here's the Trick——————

The trick is to split the two-digit number into two parts, multiply each part separately, then add the two products together. Since multiples of 10 are easy to multiply, start by splitting out a multiple of 10. Let's now multiply 13 by 8 this way to see how many people will fit on the roller coaster.

✎ **Problem:** 13×8

Step 1. Split 13 into two parts   ⟶ $13 = 10 + 3$
Step 2. Multiply the 10 by 8   ⟶ $10 \times 8 = 80$
Step 3. Multiply the 3 by 8   ⟶ $3 \times 8 = 24$
Step 4. Add the 80 and the 24   ⟶ $80 + 24 = 104$

    Answer: 104 people

✎ Let's try 24×7

Step 1. Split the 24 into two parts   ⟶ $24 = 20 + 4$
Step 2. Multiply the 20 by 7   ⟶ $20 \times 7 = 140$
Step 3. Multiply the 4 by 7   ⟶ $4 \times 7 = 28$
Step 4. Add the 140 and the 28   ⟶ $140 + 28 = 168$

    Answer: 168

FOOD FOR THOUGHT   This trick works best when multiply-ing a two-digit number by a one-digit number. You're multiplying from left to right because you begin with the tens digit and end with the ones digit. This trick takes getting used to, but it's terrific because it works with any two-digit number and any one-digit number.

_____Now It's Your Turn_____

I. $12 \times 9 = $ **108**

2. $15 \times 8 = $

3. $37 \times 3 = $

4. $26 \times 6 = $

5. $18 \times 7 = $

6. $23 \times 8 = $

(*See answers on page 140.*)

#33

League Play

Multiplying by Altering

You've just joined a Saturday-morning bowling league. There are 19 teams in the league, and each team has 5 bowlers on it. How many bowlers are there in your league? To solve this problem, you would multiply 19 by 5.

_____*Here's the Trick*_____

This trick can be used when one of the multipliers ends in 9. The trick is to add 1 to the number that ends in 9 to make it a multiple of ten. Then multiply. When you get the answer, subtract the second number to get your final answer. Now let's use the trick to see how many bowlers are on the league.

✎ **Problem:** 19 × 5

Step 1. Add 1 to the 19   ⟶   19 + 1 = 20
Step 2. Multiply 20 by 5   ⟶   20 × 5 = 100
Step 3. Subtract 5 from the 100   ⟶   100 − 5 = 95

    Answer: 95 bowlers

✎ Let's try this trick out on 39 × 4

Step 1. Add 1 to the 39   ⟶   39 + 1 = 40
Step 2. Multiply 40 by 4   ⟶   40 × 4 = 160
Step 3. Subtract 4 from the 160   ⟶   160 − 4 = 156

    Answer: 156

FOOD FOR THOUGHT This trick works because adding 1 to one number means that you end up multiplying the second number one too many times. So all you have to do is subtract it at the end.

_____*Now It's Your Turn*_____

1. $19 \times 4 = $ **76**
2. $49 \times 3 = $
3. $29 \times 5 = $

4. $39 \times 6 = $
5. $19 \times 8 = $
6. $69 \times 3 = $

(See answers on page 140.)

#34

Tilting at Windmills

Multiplying Two Numbers Just Over 100

You're traveling cross-country with your family, and you spot an enormous field of windmills. These windmills supply electricity to nearby towns. In all, there are 102 by 107 rows of windmills. How many windmills are there altogether? To solve this problem, you would multiply 102 by 107.

_____***Here's the Trick***_____

You can use this trick to multiply numbers from 101 through 109. In each case, the answer will be a five-digit number beginning with 1. The next two digits of the answer will equal the *sum* of the ones digits. The last two digits of the answer will equal the *product* of the ones digits. A sum or product of one digit, such as 4, is written as two digits, or 04. Let's use this trick to see how many windmills are at work.

✎ **Problem:** 102 × 107

Step 1. Begin the answer with 1 ⟶ 1
Step 2. Add the ones digits ⟶ 2 + 7 = 09
Step 3. Multiply the ones digits ⟶ 2 × 7 = 14
Step 4. Combine the amounts from steps 1, 2, and 3, writing from left to right ⟶ 10,914

Answer: 10,914 windmills

✎ Let's look at one more example: 109 × 104

Step 1. Begin the answer with 1 ⟶ 1
Step 2. Add the ones digits ⟶ 9 + 4 = 13
Step 3. Multiply the ones digits ⟶ 9 × 4 = 36
Step 4. Combine the amounts from steps 1, 2, and 3, writing from left to right ⟶ 11,336

Answer: 11,336

FOOD FOR THOUGHT In *some* cases, this trick will also work when one of the numbers to multiply is greater than 109. But it will *always* work on numbers from 101 through 109.

_____Now It's Your Turn_____

1. $101 \times 101 = $ **10,201**
2. $108 \times 103 = $
3. $105 \times 105 = $

4. $104 \times 107 = $
5. $106 \times 102 = $
6. $109 \times 109 = $

(See answers on page 140.)

#35

Newspaper Route

Cross-Multiplication

To earn money, you've been delivering newspapers every day for the past few months. All of your 22 customers receive a newspaper seven days a week. How many newspapers did you deliver during the month of May alone? To solve this problem, you would multiply 22 by 31, since there are 31 days in May.

―――――――――――*Here's the Trick*―――――――――――

You'll impress others by writing down the answer without showing any work. First, multiply the ones digits together and put the result in the ones place of the answer. Then, "cross-multiply" by multiplying the ones digit of each number by the tens digit of the other, and adding the result. Put this in the tens place of the answer. Finally, multiply the tens digits together and put the result in the hundreds place of the answer. Make sure to carry whenever a product is greater than 9. Let's use this trick to see how many newspapers you delivered during May.

✎ **Problem:** 22×31

Step 1. Multiply the
ones digits → $2 \times 1 = 2$ (ones-digit answer)

Step 2. Cross-multiply
and add → $(2 \times 1) + (2 \times 3) = 8$ (tens-digit answer)

Step 3. Multiply the
tens digits → $2 \times 3 = 6$ (hundreds-digit answer)

Answer: 682 newspapers (see below)

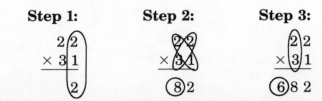

✎ Let's try one more cross-multiplication: 41×23

Step 1:

Step 2:

Step 3:

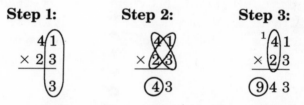

[Note: In step 2, the answer equals 14. We write down the 4 and carry the 1 to step 3.]

FOOD FOR THOUGHT This trick will work when multiplying any two-digit numbers. It will also work for larger numbers, but the cross-multiplication becomes more complicated.

—————————*Now It's Your Turn*—————————

1. 13	2. 21	3. 15	4. 46	5. 24	6. 33
× 21	× 14	× 62	× 11	× 53	× 41
273					

(*See answers on page 140.*)

#36
Feeding Time
Dividing with Decimal Points

You just bought a 36-ounce bag of food for your pet hamster named Hamlet. Every day Hamlet eats 1.2 ounces of hamster food. How many days will go by before you'll have to buy another bag? To solve this problem, you would divide 36 by 1.2.

―――――――――**Here's the Trick**――――――――

In trick #26, you learned to multiply with decimals by leaving out the decimal point when starting the problem. Then you put the decimal point back (when necessary) to finish the problem. To divide with decimals do exactly the same thing, except that you may have to tack on a zero or two to finish the problem. Now let's take 36 ÷ 1.2 and see how long before we have to buy more pet food.

✎ **Problem:** 36 ÷ 1.2

Step 1. Rewrite the problem, without the
            decimal point ―――――――――――――――▶ 36 ÷ 12
Step 2. Divide 36 by 12 ―――――――――――――▶ 36 ÷ 12 = 3
Step 3. Put a zero after the 3 (see Time-Out
            below) ――――――――――――――――――▶ 30

   Answer: 30 days

Time-Out: After performing step 2 above, ask yourself, "Does 3 seem to be the answer to 36 ÷ 1.2?" No, that's much too small. What if we tack on a zero and make it 30? Yes, that's more like it, and that's how many days our bag of food will last.

Now It's Your Turn

I. $48 \div 2.4 =$ **20**

2. $51 \div 1.7 =$

3. $7.5 \div 0.5 =$

4. $64 \div 1.6 =$

5. $77 \div 1.1 =$

6. $125 \div 2.5 =$

(See answers on page 140.)

#37

The School Picnic

Dividing by 25

The big event of the year is the school picnic in May. Everybody always shows up, and there's always lots of food. The person who buys the food for the picnic expects 600 slices of watermelon to be eaten. If the average watermelon is cut into 25 slices, how many watermelons must be bought? To solve this problem, you would divide 600 by 25.

_____*Here's the Trick*_____

We're going to divide a number by 25 in two steps. First, divide the number by 100 (lop off two zeroes, or move the decimal point to the left two places). Then, multiply by 4. Let's use this trick to see how many watermelons are needed for the picnic.

✎ **Problem:** 600 ÷ 25

Step 1. Divide 600 by 100 ⟶ 600 ÷ 100 = 6
Step 2. Multiply the 6 by 4 ⟶ 6 × 4 = 24

    Answer: 24 watermelons

✎ Let's look at one more example: 120 ÷ 25

Step 1. Divide 120 by 100 ⟶ 120 ÷ 100 = 1.20
                                                (or 1.2)
Step 2. Multiply the 1.2 by 4 ⟶ 1.2 × 4 = 4.8

    Answer: 4.8

FOOD FOR THOUGHT Step 1 (dividing by 100) can be done in a flash. Step 2 (multiplying by 4) can be done by doubling, and then doubling again (remember trick #8?).

_____*Now It's Your Turn*_____

I. $700 \div 25 = $ **28**
2. $110 \div 25 =$
3. $900 \div 25 =$

4. $80 \div 25 =$
5. $1{,}300 \div 25 =$
6. $400 \div 25 =$

(See answers on page 140.)

#38

Music, Music, Music

Dividing by Splitting

Y̵our older sister is a musician with a five-piece rock band. On Saturday night her band has a job which pays $115 per hour. If the $115 is divided evenly among the five musicians, how much will each person earn per hour? To solve this problem, you would divide 115 by 5.

_____*Here's the Trick*_____

This trick is easiest to use when the number being divided is a little over 100. To speed up the calculation, split the number being divided into two parts so that one part is 100. Then divide both parts of the number by the second number and add the results. Let's use this method to see how much your sister is earning per hour.

✎ **Problem:** 115 ÷ 5

Step 1. Split 115 into 100 and 15 ⟶ 115 = 100 + 15
Step 2. Divide 100 by 5 ⟶ 100 ÷ 5 = 20
Step 3. Divide 15 by 5 ⟶ 15 ÷ 5 = 3
Step 4. Add the 20 and the 3 ⟶ 20 + 3 = 23

    Answer: $23 per hour

✎ Let's look at one more example: 112 ÷ 4

Step 1. Split 112 into 100 and 12 ⟶ 112 = 100 + 12
Step 2. Divide 100 by 4 ⟶ 100 ÷ 4 = 25
Step 3. Divide 12 by 4 ⟶ 12 ÷ 4 = 3
Step 4. Add the 25 and the 3 ⟶ 25 + 3 = 28

    Answer: 28

FOOD FOR THOUGHT   This trick will work when dividing, let's say, 165 by 5, even though 165 is more than just a little over 100. It would just take a bit longer to solve than the examples above.

──────────*Now It's Your Turn*──────────

1. 112 ÷ 2 = **56**
2. 125 ÷ 5 =
3. 116 ÷ 4 =

4. 118 ÷ 2 =
5. 135 ÷ 5 =
6. 132 ÷ 4 =

(See answers on page 140.)

#39

Say "Cheese"

Dividing by Altering

Someone has given you a new camera, and you're taking picture after picture. Eventually, you have four rolls of film developed and get back 96 pictures. If the rolls took the same number of pictures, how many pictures did each roll take? To solve this problem, you would divide 96 by 4.

_____*Here's the Trick*_____

This trick is easiest to use when the number being divided is a little under 100. Think of the number being divided as 100 minus something. So 96, for example, becomes $100 - 4$. Perform division on the two parts (for example, on the 100 and the 4), and then subtract. Let's use this method to see how many pictures you took with each roll.

✎ **Problem:** $96 \div 4$

Step 1. Think of 96 as $100 - 4$ ⟶ $96 = 100 - 4$
Step 2. Divide 100 by 4   ⟶ $100 \div 4 = 25$
Step 3. Divide 4 by 4   ⟶ $4 \div 4 = 1$
Step 4. Subtract the 1 from the 25   ⟶ $25 - 1 = 24$

    Answer: 24 pictures

✎ Let's look at one more example: $90 \div 5$

Step 1. Think of 90 as $100 - 10$ ⟶ $90 = 100 - 10$
Step 2. Divide 100 by 5   ⟶ $100 \div 5 = 20$
Step 3. Divide 10 by 5   ⟶ $10 \div 5 = 2$
Step 4. Subtract the 2 from the 20   ⟶ $20 - 2 = 18$

    Answer: 18

FOOD FOR THOUGHT   This trick will work when dividing, let's say, 76 by 4, even though 76 is well under 100. It would just take a bit longer to solve than the examples above.

———————————*Now It's Your Turn*———————————

1. 96 ÷ 2 = **48**
2. 95 ÷ 5 =
3. 92 ÷ 4 =

4. 98 ÷ 2 =
5. 85 ÷ 5 =
6. 94 ÷ 2 =

(See answers on page 141.)

#40

Railroad Crossing

Dividing with Even Numbers

You're riding on the bus and all of a sudden you must stop because a train is coming. It looks like a very long, slow train, and you're wondering how long you'll have to wait at the railroad crossing. There are 126 railroad cars, and 14 cars pass every minute. How many minutes will you have to wait? To solve this problem, you would divide 126 by 14.

─────────────────*Here's the Trick*─────────────────

Whenever both numbers of a division problem are even, you can simplify the calculation by cutting each number in half. If two even numbers result, cut those in half as well. When one of the numbers becomes odd, then solve the problem. Let's use this trick to see how long the train will take to pass.

✎ **Problem:** 126 ÷ 14

Step 1. Divide 126 by 2 ⟶ $126 ÷ 2 = 63$
Step 2. Divide 14 by 2 ⟶ $14 ÷ 2 = 7$
Step 3. Divide 63 by 7 ⟶ $63 ÷ 7 = 9$

    Answer: 9 minutes

✎ Let's look at one more example: 84 ÷ 8

Step 1. Divide 84 by 2 ⟶ $84 ÷ 2 = 42$
Step 2. Divide 8 by 2 ⟶ $8 ÷ 2 = 4$

[You now have 42 ÷ 4, so you can cut those numbers in half.]

Step 3. Divide 42 by 2 ⟶ $42 ÷ 2 = 21$
Step 4. Divide 4 by 2 ⟶ $4 ÷ 2 = 2$
Step 5. Divide 21 by 2 ⟶ $21 ÷ 2 = 10.5$

    Answer: 10.5

FOOD FOR THOUGHT This trick won't always work out as nicely as it does above, but it will produce smaller numbers, which are usually easier to work with.

_____*Now It's Your Turn*_____

1. $78 \div 6 = 39 \div 3 =$ **13**
2. $144 \div 12 =$
3. $68 \div 4 =$

4. $124 \div 8 =$
5. $84 \div 6 =$
6. $200 \div 16 =$

(*See answers on page 141.*)

ESTIMATION
TRICKS

_____*A Brief Word about Estimating*_____

One of the most valuable math skills you can learn is rapid estimation. Every day we must produce "ballpark figures," or estimates, on the spot. When estimating multiplication and division, you must be very careful or your estimate will be way off. All of the next eight multiplication and division tricks were carefully chosen, and will produce an estimate that is within ½ of 1 percent to 2 percent of the true answer (which is a pretty good estimate!).

#41

Dinosaur Bones

Estimating Multiplication by 33 or 34

You're at the museum of natural history, looking at all the dinosaur skeletons. The one in front of you is 33 feet high. Approximately how many inches is that? To solve this problem, you would estimate multiplication of 33 by 12, since there are 12 inches in a foot.

───────────────*Here's the Trick*───────────────

Multiplying by 33 or 34 takes a while to do. But to *estimate* multiplication by 33 or 34, simply divide the other number by 3, and multiply the result by 100. Let's use this trick to see approximately how high our dinosaur is.

✎ **Problem:** Estimate 33 × 12

Step 1. Divide 12 by 3 ──────────► 12 ÷ 3 = 4
Step 2. Multiply 4 by 100 ──────────► 4 × 100 = 400

   Answer: Approximately 400 inches high

✎ Let's look at one more example: Estimate 21 × 34

Step 1. Divide 21 by 3 ──────────► 21 ÷ 3 = 7
Step 2. Multiply 7 by 100 ──────────► 7 × 100 = 700

   Answer: Approximately 700

FOOD FOR THOUGHT   The actual answer to 12 × 33 (our first example) is 396, or 1 percent lower than our estimate of 400. The actual answer to 21 × 34 (our second example) is 714, or 2 percent higher than our estimate of 700. Those are pretty close estimates!

_____*Now It's Your Turn*_____

(Note: The symbol ≈ means "approximately equals.")

1. 24 × 33 ≈ **800 (exact answer = 792)**
2. 18 × 34 ≈
3. 42 × 33 ≈
4. 39 × 34 ≈
5. 66 × 33 ≈
6. 75 × 34 ≈

(See answers on page 141.)

#42

Car Trek

Estimating Multiplication by 49 or 51

You're about to take a long trip by car. Your family has an economy car which will drive approximately 49 miles on one gallon of gasoline. If the gas tank holds 14 gallons, approximately how many miles can you drive on one tankful of gas? To solve this problem, you would estimate multiplication of 14 by 49.

_____*Here's the Trick*_____

Multiplying by 49 or 51 is difficult and time consuming. But to *estimate* multiplication by 49 or 51, simply divide the other number by 2, and multiply the result by 100. Let's use this trick to see approximately how many miles you can travel on one tankful of gas.

✎ **Problem:** Estimate 14 × 49

Step 1. Divide 14 by 2 $\longrightarrow$ 14 ÷ 2 = 7
Step 2. Multiply 7 by 100 $\longrightarrow$ 7 × 100 = 700

 Answer: Approximately 700 miles

✎ Let's look at one more example: Estimate 26 × 51

Step 1. Divide 26 by 2 $\longrightarrow$ 26 ÷ 2 = 13
Step 2. Multiply 13 by 100 $\longrightarrow$ 13 × 100 = 1,300

 Answer: Approximately 1,300

FOOD FOR THOUGHT The actual answer to 14 × 49 (our first example) is 686, or 2 percent under our estimate of 700. The actual answer to 26 × 51 (our second example) is 1,326, or 2 percent over our estimate of 1,300.

───────────*Now It's Your Turn*───────────

1. 32 × 49 ≈ **1,600**
   (exact answer = 1,568)

2. 18 × 51 ≈

3. 56 × 49 ≈

4. 44 × 51 ≈

5. 72 × 49 ≈

6. 94 × 51 ≈

(See answers on page 141.)

#43

Car Trek II

Estimating Multiplication by 66 or 67

Remember the long trip you were about to take in our last chapter? Well, let's say you rode 12 hours during the first day. You averaged 66 miles per hour on the open highway. Approximately how many miles did you travel that first day? To solve this problem, you would estimate multiplication of 12 by 66.

───────────────*Here's the Trick*───────────────

To estimate multiplication by 66 or 67, multiply the other number by ²/₃, then multiply the result by 100. To multiply a number by ²/₃, take ¹/₃ of the number, then double it. Let's use this trick to see approximately how many miles you've traveled.

✎ **Problem:** Estimate 12 × 66

Step 1. Multiply 12 by ²/₃ by taking $\rightarrow$ $\begin{cases} 12 \times \frac{1}{3} = 4 \\ 4 \times 2 = 8 \end{cases}$
  ¹/₃ of 12 and doubling it
Step 2. Multiply 8 by 100 $\longrightarrow$ 8 × 100 = 800

  Answer: Approximately 800 miles

✎ Let's look at one more example: Estimate 9 × 67

Step 1. Multiply 9 by ²/₃ by taking $\rightarrow$ $\begin{cases} 9 \times \frac{1}{3} = 3 \\ 3 \times 2 = 6 \end{cases}$
  ¹/₃ of 9 and doubling it
Step 2. Multiply 6 by 100 $\longrightarrow$ 6 × 100 = 600

  Answer: Approximately 600

FOOD FOR THOUGHT The actual answer to 12 × 66 (our first example) is 792, or 1 percent under our estimate of 800. The actual answer to 9 × 67 (our second example) is 603, or ½ of 1 percent over our estimate of 600.

_____*Now It's Your Turn*_____

1. 18 × 66 ≈ **1,200**   4. 39 × 67 ≈
    (exact answer = 1,188)
2. 27 × 67 ≈   5. 75 × 66 ≈
3. 42 × 66 ≈   6. 21 × 67 ≈

(See answers on page 141.)

#44

Car Trek III:
The Voyage Home
Estimating Division by 33 or 34

You've enjoyed your vacation, but all good things must come to an end. To make the ride home go faster, you decide to finish that novel you brought with you. You have 150 pages to go and can read about 33 pages per hour. Approximately how many hours will it take you to finish it? To solve this problem, you would estimate division of 150 by 33.

_____*Here's the Trick*_____

To estimate division by 33 or 34, divide the other number by 100, then multiply the result by 3. Let's use this trick to see about how long it will be until you finish your novel.

✎ **Problem:** Estimate $150 \div 33$

Step 1. Divide 150 by 100 ———➤ $150 \div 100 = 1.5$
Step 2. Multiply 1.5 by 3 ———➤ $1.5 \times 3 = 4.5$ (or $4\frac{1}{2}$)

    Answer: About $4\frac{1}{2}$ hours

✎ Let's look at one more example: Estimate $240 \div 34$

Step 1. Divide 240 by 100 ———➤ $240 \div 100 = 2.4$
Step 2. Multiply 2.4 by 3 ———➤ $2.4 \times 3 = 7.2$

    Answer: Approximately 7.2

FOOD FOR THOUGHT The actual answer to 150 ÷ 33 (our first example) is about 4.55, or about 1 percent over our estimate of 4.5. The actual answer to 240 ÷ 34 (our second example) is about 7.06, or about 2 percent under our estimate of 7.2.

———————Now It's Your Turn———————

1. 800 ÷ 33 ≈ **24**
   (**exact answer = 24.2424 . . .**)
2. 160 ÷ 34 ≈
3. 220 ÷ 33 ≈

4. 700 ÷ 34 ≈

5. 250 ÷ 33 ≈
6. 310 ÷ 34 ≈

(*See answers on page 141.*)

#45

Sorting Things Out

Estimating Division by 49 or 51

It's amazing how many letters are delivered by the U.S. Post Office every day. With the help of machines, postal workers can sort millions of pieces of mail a day. Let's say that one postal worker can sort 49 letters per minute. Approximately how many minutes will it take that worker to sort 800 letters? To solve this problem, you would estimate division of 800 by 49.

—————————————*Here's the Trick*—————————————

To estimate division by 49 or 51, divide the other number by 100, then multiply the result by 2. Let's use this trick to see how long it will take to sort those letters.

✎ **Problem:** Estimate 800 ÷ 49

Step 1. Divide 800 by 100 ——————▶ $800 \div 100 = 8$
Step 2. Multiply 8 by 2 ——————▶ $8 \times 2 = 16$

   Answer: About 16 minutes

✎ Let's look at one more example: Estimate 640 ÷ 51

Step 1. Divide 640 by 100 ——————▶ $640 \div 100 = 6.4$
Step 2. Multiply 6.4 by 2 ——————▶ $6.4 \times 2 = 12.8$

   Answer: Approximately 12.8

FOOD FOR THOUGHT   The actual answer to 800 ÷ 49 (our first example) is about 16.33, or about 2 percent over our estimate of 16. The actual answer to 640 ÷ 51 (our second example) is about 12.55, or about 2 percent below our estimate of 12.8.

Now It's Your Turn

1. 700 ÷ 49 ≈ **14**
   (exact answer is about 14.3)

2. 450 ÷ 51 ≈

3. 320 ÷ 49 ≈

4. 180 ÷ 51 ≈

5. 910 ÷ 49 ≈

6. 270 ÷ 51 ≈

(See answers on page 141.)

#46

Field-Trip Fun

Estimating Division by 66 or 67

You've been looking forward to this day for a long time. Your entire school is going on a field trip to the planetarium. In all, there are 400 students at your school. If each bus can hold 66 students, approximately how many buses will be needed to make the trip? To solve this problem, you would estimate division of 400 by 66.

_____*Here's the Trick*_____

To estimate division by 66 or 67, divide the other number by 100, then multiply by 1.5 (1½). Let's use this trick to see about how many buses will be needed for the field trip.

✎ **Problem:** Estimate 400 ÷ 66

Step 1. Divide 400 by 100 ——————→ 400 ÷ 100 = 4
Step 2. Multiply 4 by 1.5 ——————→ 4 × 1.5 = 6

   Answer: Approximately 6 buses

(Note that the answer to our field trip question is *approximately* 6 buses. Six buses multiplied by 66 students equals 396 students. If all 400 students show up that day, 4 will not be able to get on any of those six buses! This is why an estimate isn't always good enough.)

✎ Let's look at one more example: Estimate 120 ÷ 67

Step 1. Divide 120 by 100 ——————→ 120 ÷ 100 = 1.2
Step 2. Multiply 1.2 by 1.5 ——————→ 1.2 × 1.5 = 1.8

   Answer: 1.8

TO ESTIMATE DIVISION BY 66 OR 67, JUST DIVIDE BY 100, THEN MULTIPLY BY 1.5 (1½), AND THE SKY'S THE LIMIT!

FOOD FOR THOUGHT Multiplying a number by 1.5 (1½) means taking the number and adding half again. To multiply 14 by 1.5, add 14 to half of 14 (or 7), which equals 21.

───────────*Now It's Your Turn*───────────

1. 500 ÷ 66 ≈ **7.5**
    (exact answer is about 7.6)
2. 800 ÷ 67 ≈
3. 700 ÷ 66 ≈

4. 180 ÷ 67 ≈
5. 2,000 ÷ 66 ≈
6. 3,200 ÷ 67 ≈

(See answers on page 142.)

#47

Home-Run Derby

Estimating Division by 9

You've just played a softball game that lasted nine innings. In all, your team scored a whopping 35 runs. On the average, about how many runs did your team score per inning? To solve this problem, you would estimate division of 35 by 9.

_____*Here's the Trick*_____

To estimate division by 9, multiply the other number by 11, then divide the result by 100. You may remember from trick #10 how to quickly multiply a two-digit number by 11: Add the two digits of the number and place the sum in the middle of the original two digits. (You have to carry when the digits total more than 9.) So 35 × 11 = 3 (3 + 5) 5, or 385. Let's use this trick to see about how many runs you averaged per inning.

✎ **Problem:** Estimate 35 ÷ 9

Step 1. Multiply 35 by 11 ⟶ 35 × 11 = 385
Step 2. Divide 385 by 100 ⟶ 385 ÷ 100 = 3.85

   Answer: Approximately 3.85 (or just under 4) runs per inning!

✎ Let's look at one more example: Estimate 76 ÷ 9

Step 1. Multiply 76 by 11 ⟶ 76 × 11 = 836
Step 2. Divide 836 by 100 ⟶ 836 ÷ 100 = 8.36

   Answer: Approximately 8.36

FOOD FOR THOUGHT   This trick has you multiplying by 11 to divide by 9. You'll see that our next trick has you multiplying by 9 to divide by 11. The key numbers for these two tricks are 9 and 11. They are easy to remember because 9 × 11 = 99.

_____*Now It's Your Turn*_____

1.   51 ÷ 9 ≈ **5.61**
     (exact answer = 5.666 . . .)
2.   62 ÷ 9 ≈
3.   40 ÷ 9 ≈

4.   70 ÷ 9 ≈

5.   85 ÷ 9 ≈
6.   69 ÷ 9 ≈

(See answers on page 142.)

#48

The Jog-a-Thon

Estimating Division by 11

You and ten of your friends have entered a jog-a-thon to help raise money for a worthy cause. The more miles you jog, the more money will go to charity. The 11 of you have set a goal to jog a total of 50 miles. On the average, approximately how many miles would each of you have to jog? To solve this problem, you would estimate division of 50 by 11.

_____*Here's the Trick*_____

To estimate division by 11, multiply the other number by 9, then divide the result by 100. (Trick #27 in this book shows how to multiply by 9 quickly.) Let's use this trick to see about how many miles each of you must jog.

✎ **Problem:** Estimate 50 ÷ 11

Step 1. Multiply 50 by 9 ⟶ $50 \times 9 = 450$
Step 2. Divide 450 by 100 ⟶ $450 \div 100 = 4.5$

 Answer: About 4.5 (or 4½) miles

✎ Let's look at one more example: Estimate 400 ÷ 11

Step 1. Multiply 400 by 9 ⟶ $400 \times 9 = 3{,}600$
Step 2. Divide 3,600 by 100 ⟶ $3{,}600 \div 100 = 36$

 Answer: Approximately 36

FOOD FOR THOUGHT   In the example above, it might have been easier to first divide by 100, and then multiply by 9. Whatever the calculation, this trick will give you an estimate that is within about 1 percent of the true answer.

————————Now It's Your Turn————————

1. $90 \div 11 \approx$ **8.1**
    (exact answer is about 8.2)
2. $60 \div 11 \approx$
3. $200 \div 11 \approx$

4. $700 \div 11 \approx$

5. $300 \div 11 \approx$
6. $800 \div 11 \approx$

(See answers on page 142.)

TRICKS TO CHECK YOUR ANSWER

_____

#49

Video Mania

Checking Addition and Subtraction

Your favorite store, Video Village, sells more video games than any other store. During the past two days alone, it has sold 31 and 41 games. You think that totals 72, but you'd like to check your answer without having to add all over again. Let's see how that's done.

_____*Here's the Trick*_____

This method will tell you if you definitely have the wrong answer or if you probably have the right answer. First, you must obtain a "digit-sum" for each number you're adding. The digit-sum is the digits of the number added together. For example, the digit-sum of 35 is 8, because $3 + 5 = 8$. Only a single-digit number can be a digit-sum. So when a digit-sum is greater than 9, do another digit-sum calculation until you get a single-digit number. For example, when calculating the digit-sum of 716, you first get 14 ($7 + 1 + 6$). The digit-sum of 14 is 5 ($1 + 4$), so the digit-sum of 716 is 5. Now let's see if $31 + 41$ *probably does* or *definitely does not* equal 72.

$$
\begin{array}{ll}
31 & (\text{digit-sum} = 3 + 1 = 4) \\
+ 41 & (\text{digit-sum} = 4 + 1 = 5) \\
\hline
& (\text{add the digit-sums from above: } 4 + 5 = 9) \\
72 & (\text{digit-sum} = 7 + 2 = 9) \longleftarrow \text{compare} \longrightarrow
\end{array}
$$

Answer: Because the number you got by adding the two digit-sums matches the digit-sum of the answer (9), you *probably* have the correct answer.

FOOD FOR THOUGHT   The reason we can only say that probably 31 + 41 = 72 is that an answer of 27 or 63 would give the same
digit-sum as 72 (9), but they clearly are not the correct answer.

_____*Now It's Your Turn*_____

(For each calculation, write "probably correct" or "definitely
incorrect.")

  1.   73 + 66 = 129 **(definitely incorrect because digit-
       sums do not match)**
  2.   89 + 41 + 32 = 162
  3.   777 + 333 + 666 = 1,776
  4.   556 + 208 + 317 = 1,181
*5.   486 − 197 = 289
*6.   917 − 563 = 344

*Check subtraction problems by first turning them into addi-
tion problems, and then checking as above. So 75 − 27 = 48
could be checked as 48 + 27 = 75.

(*See answers on page 142.*)

#50

Grand Finale

Checking Multiplication and Division

Congratulations! You won a trip around the world, and are about to board your plane. It's a wide-bodied plane with 31 rows, 11 seats across. To calculate the total number of seats on the plane, you multiply 31 by 11 using the "11 trick." You'd like to check your answer, 341, but don't want to multiply all over again. Let's see how that's done.

―――――――――――*Here's the Trick*―――――――――――

First of all, make sure you understand trick #49, "Checking Addition and Subtraction." We will use the same method for multiplication and division. The only difference is that we are going to multiply digit-sums at one point. Now let's see if 31×11 *probably does* or *definitely does not* equal 341.

    31   (digit-sum = 3 + 1 = 4)
  × 11   (digit-sum = 1 + 1 = 2)
  ――――   (multiply the digit-sums from above: 4 × 2 = 8)
   341   (digit-sum = 3 + 4 + 1 = 8) ◄――― compare

Answer: Because the product of the multiplied digit-sums and the digit-sum of the answer are both 8, you *probably* have the correct answer.

✎ Let's look at one more example: $453 \times 78 = 35{,}134$

     453   (digit-sum = 12; digit-sum of 12 = 3)
   × 78   (digit-sum = 15; digit-sum of 15 = 6)
   ――――   (multiply: 3 × 6 = 18; digit-sum of 18 = 9)
  35,134 (digit-sum = 16; digit-sum of 16 = 7) ◄ compare

Answer: Because the digit-sum of the answer (7) does not match the digit-sum of the multiplied numbers (9), we *definitely* have the wrong answer (the correct answer is 35,334).

FOOD FOR THOUGHT   The reason we can only probably say that 31 × 11 = 341 is that an answer of 431 or 251 would give the same digit-sum as 341 (8), but they clearly are not the correct answer.

_____*Now It's Your Turn*_____

(For each calculation, write "probably correct" or "definitely incorrect.")

1. 83 × 47 = 3,901 **(probably correct)**
2. 91 × 66 = 6,106
3. 355 × 104 = 36,820
4. 727 × 83 = 60,341
*5. 2,064 ÷ 24 = 86
*6. 5,152 ÷ 161 = 42

*Check division problems by first turning them into multiplication problems, and then checking as above. So 2,035 ÷ 55 = 37 can be checked as 37 × 55 = 2,035.

(See answers on page 142.)

Conclusion

Congratulations! You've completed the program and are well on your way to becoming a mental-math wizard.

But remember, you don't have to use *every* trick you've learned. Just use the ones you like the most and think you'll have the easiest time remembering.

Don't be afraid to experiment and to use your imagination when doing a calculation. Whatever method gives you the correct answer the fastest is the method you should use.

You should also keep your mind "mathematically fit." When you're at a fast-food restaurant, try to figure the cost of a burger, fries, and a shake. When you see numbers on a license plate, billboard, or TV screen, try adding, subtracting, multiplying, and dividing these numbers—anything to keep your mind thinking about numbers.

I hope you enjoyed learning these arithmetricks as much as I enjoyed teaching them. I would love to receive your comments, suggestions, or perhaps a description of your very own rapid math tricks. You can write to: Professor Edward H. Julius, c/o School of Business, California Lutheran University, 60 West Olsen Road, Thousand Oaks, CA 91360.

Teachers and others—I do hold workshops for schools, businesses, and organizations on the topic of rapid calculation. Please write to me at the above address for further information.

Thank you, and good luck!

Ed Julius

Appendix A
Symbols, Terms, and Tables

Symbols

+ means "plus" or "add" or "and"
− means "minus" or "subtract" or "take away"
× means "times" or "multiplied by"
÷ means "divided by"
= means "equals"
≈ means "approximately equals" (used when estimating)
n^2 (spoken "n-squared") means a certain number multiplied by itself

Terms

ballpark test   A quick check of an answer to see if it "looks right." A ballpark test should always be performed on a calculation.

digit   A single part of a number, such as the ones-place digit. For example, there are three digits in the number 714.

estimate   To get an answer that is approximately equal to the exact answer. One estimate of 21 × 19 is 400. An estimate is also called a "ballpark figure."

even number   A number that can be divided by 2 without giving a remainder. Examples are 2, 4, 6, and 8.

multiple   The result of multiplying another number by 2, 3, 4, and so on. For example, multiples of 5 are 10, 15, 20, and so on.

odd number   A number that gives a remainder of 1 when divided by 2. Examples are 1, 3, 5, and 7.

product   The answer to a multiplication problem.

square   To multiply a number by itself.

sum   The answer to an addition problem.

whole number   A number such as 0, 1, 2, and 3.

Addition/Subtraction Table

+	1	2	3	4	5	6	7	8	9	10	11	12
1	2	3	4	5	6	7	8	9	10	11	12	13
2	3	4	5	6	7	8	9	10	11	12	13	14
3	4	5	6	7	8	9	10	11	12	13	14	15
4	5	6	7	8	9	10	11	12	13	14	15	16
5	6	7	8	9	10	11	12	13	14	15	16	17
6	7	8	9	10	11	12	13	14	15	16	17	18
7	8	9	10	11	12	13	14	15	16	17	18	19
8	9	10	11	12	13	14	15	16	17	18	19	20
9	10	11	12	13	14	15	16	17	18	19	20	21
10	11	12	13	14	15	16	17	18	19	20	21	22
11	12	13	14	15	16	17	18	19	20	21	22	23
12	13	14	15	16	17	18	19	20	21	22	23	24

Multiplication/Division Table

×	1	2	3	4	5	6	7	8	9	10	11	12
1	1	2	3	4	5	6	7	8	9	10	11	12
2	2	4	6	8	10	12	14	16	18	20	22	24
3	3	6	9	12	15	18	21	24	27	30	33	36
4	4	8	12	16	20	24	28	32	36	40	44	48
5	5	10	15	20	25	30	35	40	45	50	55	60
6	6	12	18	24	30	36	42	48	54	60	66	72
7	7	14	21	28	35	42	49	56	63	70	77	84
8	8	16	24	32	40	48	56	64	72	80	88	96
9	9	18	27	36	45	54	63	72	81	90	99	108
10	10	20	30	40	50	60	70	80	90	100	110	120
11	11	22	33	44	55	66	77	88	99	110	121	132
12	12	24	36	48	60	72	84	96	108	120	132	144

Some Squares You Should Know

$1^2 = 1$	$6^2 = 36$	$11^2 = 121$
$2^2 = 4$	$7^2 = 49$	$12^2 = 144$
$3^2 = 9$	$8^2 = 64$	$13^2 = 169$
$4^2 = 16$	$9^2 = 81$	$14^2 = 196$
$5^2 = 25$	$10^2 = 100$	$15^2 = 225$

Table of Equivalencies

Fraction	Decimal Equivalent	Fraction	Decimal Equivalent
$1/100$	0.01	$2/5$	0.4
$1/50$	0.02	$1/2$	0.5
$1/25$	0.04	$3/5$	0.6
$1/20$	0.05	$2/3$	0.666 . . .
$1/10$	0.1	$3/4$	0.75
$1/5$	0.2	$4/5$	0.8
$1/4$	0.25	n/n	1.0
$1/3$	0.333 . . .		

Appendix B

Some Dynamite Parlor Tricks

"I'd Like to Speak to The Wizard"

Here is the greatest parlor trick of them all. Have someone pick a playing card and say what the card is out loud for you and everyone else to hear. You then tell your guests that you know someone, known as "The Wizard," who will tell them, by phone, which card was picked.

Pick up the phone and dial the wizard's phone number. When someone answers, say, "I'd like to speak to the wizard." Pause and say, "Hello, Wizard?" Pause again, and say, "There's someone who would like to speak to you." Give the phone to the person who chose the card, and the wizard will tell him or her exactly which card was chosen.

Before making the phone call, tell everyone *exactly* what you are going to say to the wizard, and do not change these words. This way, your friends will know that it isn't the wording that's telling the wizard which card was picked.

At this point, it might be fun for you to try to figure out how the trick is done. If you can't figure it out, read on.

———————Here's the Trick———————

As you may have guessed, the "wizard" is just a friend or relative who knows exactly what to do when he or she picks up the phone and hears the words, "I'd like to speak to the wizard."

If the person who answers the phone is not the wizard, have that person put the wizard on the phone right away. Then the wizard will start to say over the phone, "Ace, two, three . . ." and so on, all the way up to "jack, queen, king." What you do is

123

cut in and say, "Hello, Wizard?" just as the wizard says the correct card number.

After you've said, "Hello, Wizard," the wizard will say, "Spades, clubs, hearts, diamonds." You should cut in and say, "There's someone who would like to speak to you" just as the wizard has said the suit of the card chosen. The wizard will now know both the card number and the suit. You are the only one who is allowed to listen to what the wizard is saying before he or she tells your friends what card was chosen.

This trick does take a little bit of practice. For example, the wizard should not read off the card numbers and suits too fast or too slow. Once you get the hang of it, this parlor trick never fails to work and amuse!

The Amazing Missing-Digit Trick

There are a few different ways to perform this trick. Here is the easiest way.

Ask someone (your subject) to write down the number 999. Then have him or her multiply it by any three-digit number. Be sure to have a calculator handy! You will be the only one in the room that won't know what the chosen number or product is (turn your back or wear a blindfold).

Then ask your subject to circle any digit of the product, from 1 to 9 (but not 0). The subject will then read off slowly, and in random order, all the *other* digits of the product. You will then tell everyone which digit was circled (left out).

Here's the Trick

The sum of the product's digits will always be a multiple of 9 (or 9, 18, 27, and so on). As the subject is reading off the digits, you should be adding them up. The missing digit is the one that will put the sum at a multiple of 9.

Let's take an example. Your subject has multiplied 999 by 285, which equals 284,715. He then circles the digit "4." Slowly, he reads off the other five digits. You add them in your head, and they total 23. The next multiple of 9 is 27. You subtract 23 from 27, and you have the missing digit—4!

The Astounding Fifth-Root Trick

What is the fifth root of a number? It's much like the square root, only taken a few steps further. For example, $7^5 = 7 \times 7 \times 7 \times 7 \times 7$, which equals 16,807. So the fifth root of 16,807 is 7. Similarly, $24^5 = 24 \times 24 \times 24 \times 24 \times 24$, which equals 7,962,624. So the fifth root of 7,962,624 is 24.

Ask someone to multiply a whole number (from 1 to 99) by itself five times, as shown above. You'll need a 10-digit calculator for this trick. Don't watch as your volunteer is doing the calculation, but write down the final product. In a few seconds, you will astound your audience by figuring out the fifth root of that product.

_____Here's the Trick_____

Let's say your volunteer has picked a number, multiplied it out, and gives you the product 69,343,957. Right away, you will know that the ones digit of the fifth root is 7, because the product above ends in 7.

Next, ignore (or cross out) the four digits to the left of the ones digit (the 5, 9, 3, and 4). Now concentrate on the digits that remain—6 9 3. This is how the product should look to you at this point—6 9 , 3 4 3 , 9 5 7.

To figure out the tens digit of the fifth root, you'll need to have the following information memorized:
- If no number remains, then the answer is a one-digit number.
- If the remaining number (693, in our case) is in the following range: Then the tens digit is:

Range	Tens digit
1–30	1
30–230	2
230–1,000	3
1,000–3,000	4
3,000–7,500	5
7,500–16,000	6
16,000–32,000	7
32,000–57,000	8
57,000–99,000	9

Because the number 693 is in the 230–1,000 range, the tens digit is a 3. Therefore, the fifth root of 69,343,957 is 37. You might be wondering what to do if the remaining number is, for example, 230. Will the tens digit be 2 or 3? You don't have to worry, because the remaining number will never be any of the border numbers.

When using the above ranges, it might be easiest to count off each number with your fingers as follows: 1-30-230-1,000, and so on, until you reach the range with the remaining number. For example, we would have counted 1-30-230 in the above example, indicating a tens digit of 3. (We stop at 230 because the next number in the series, 1,000, is greater than our remaining number, 693.)

Let's look at one more example: Find the fifth root of 7,339,040,224. You know that the ones digit of the answer is 4. Crossing out the next four digits, the remaining number is 73,390. Looking at the above ranges, you can see that the tens digit is 9. So the fifth root of the above number is 94.

This is a terrific parlor trick, but it takes practice and memorization. You've got to know those number ranges like the back of your hand. Once you've mastered the trick, however, your audience will watch in amazement as you figure out the fifth root in only a matter of seconds!

Appendix C

Fascinating and Fun-Filled Facts about Numbers

_____*Number Knowledge*_____

Do you know the names of the numbers, starting with one thousand (1,000) and increasing one thousandfold (adding three more zeroes) each time? **Answer:**

Thousand (1,000)
Million (1,000,000)
Billion (1,000,000,000)
Trillion (1,000,000,000,000)
Quadrillion (1,000,000,000,000,000)
Quintillion (1,000,000,000,000,000,000)
Sextillion (1,000,000,000,000,000,000,000)
Septillion (1,000,000,000,000,000,000,000,000)
Octillion (1,000,000,000,000,000,000,000,000,000)
Nonillion (1,000,000,000,000,000,000,000,000,000,000)
Decillion (1,000,000,000,000,000,000,000,000,000,000,000)
and so forth

(*Note:* Although these are the names used in the United States and elsewhere, not all countries use the same names for the same numbers!)

Number Madness 1

Here's a strange one. Take any number, any number at all, and subtract the sum of the number's digits. What you'll get without fail is an answer that can be divided evenly by 9. For example, take the number 736. The sum of the digits (7 + 3 + 6) is 16. Subtract 16 from 736, and you get 720, which can be divided evenly by 9 (720 ÷ 9 = 80 exactly). Note *also* that the digit-sum of our number 720 (7 + 2 + 0) is 9!

Number Madness 2

The number "one googol," which is 10,000,000,000,000,000,000, 000,000,000,000,000,000,000,000,000,000,000,000,000, 000,000,000,000,000,000,000,000,000,000,000,000, can easily be written but couldn't be counted to in a million lifetimes. It is a number so large it is estimated that there aren't even that many atoms in the universe. However, the number "one googolplex," which is a one followed by a googol of zeroes, not only couldn't be counted to in a million lifetimes, it couldn't even be written in that same span of time!

This One's Hard to Believe

Jot down any number of any size. Then rearrange the digits in any way to form another number. Subtract the smaller number from the larger, and the digits of the result will always add up to 9, or a multiple of 9 (and will, therefore, be evenly divisible by 9). Take the number 8,174, and rearrange it as 1,847. Subtract 1,847 from 8,174 and you've got 6,327, whose digits total 18, and which is evenly divisible by 9!

Birthday Fun

How many people would you have to put in a room where the likelihood is about 50% (or ½) that at least two people share the same birthday?   **Answer:** 23 people

For Your Information

What is a prime number? It's a number, such as 3, 11, or 29, that cannot be divided evenly by any whole number other than itself and 1. What's the highest known prime number? It's a number so large it contains over 258,000 digits!

Triple Your Speed

This multiplication tip works when one of the numbers contains a repeating digit (numbers such as 222 or 77). Let's multiply 555 by 837. Then let's reverse the calculation (make it 837 × 555) and see which way is faster.

555	837
× 837	× 555
3885	4185
1665	4185
4440	4185
464,535	464,535

Can you see why the calculation on the right (837 × 555) is easier to perform than the one on the left? All you have to do is multiply 837 by 5 once, and then copy the 4,185 twice. The multiplication on the left, on the other hand, requires three separate calculations.

_____*The Mysterious Number 9*_____

When dividing a number by 9, there's a really easy way to figure out (before doing the calculation) what the remainder will be. All you have to do is add the digits of the number you're dividing by 9. For example, the remainder when taking 23 ÷ 9 is 5, because 2 + 3 = 5 (so 23 ÷ 9 = 2 r5). Sometimes the digits of the number total *more* than 9. When this happens, just add one more time. For example, when taking 67 ÷ 9, the remainder will be 4 because 6 + 7 = 13, and 1 + 3 = 4 (so 67 ÷ 9 = 7 r4). Sometimes the digits of the number total 9 or a multiple of 9 (such as 18 or 27). In these cases, there *is* no remainder.

_____*Number Challenge*_____

Think fast! Add the following numbers out loud, in order, and as quickly as you can.

1,000 + 40 + 1,000 + 30 + 1,000 + 20 + 1,000 + 10 = ?

Answer: 4,100 (not 5,000, as the majority of people obtain)

_____*Quick Trick*_____

Can you figure out a quick way to multiply any two-digit number by 101? For example, how could you instantly get the answer to 47 × 101?

Answer: Simply write the number you are multiplying by 101 *twice*. For example, 47 × 101 = 4,747.

Mathematical Note

Let's say there are nine people (or 90 fingers) in front of a piano, and they have been asked to play all possible sounds from the piano's 88 keys. They can together play any number of keys, from only 1 to all 88. Assuming they can play one different sound per second, how long will it take to play all possible combinations of keys?

Answer: About 9.8 quintillion years (that's 700 million times the estimated age of the universe!)

Just for Fun

One of the most difficult tasks in writing this book was to figure out the best order for the 50 math tricks. How would you calculate the number of different ways the 50 tricks could have been arranged?

Answer: If you were figuring out the number of different ways, say, six books could be arranged on a shelf, you would take $1 \times 2 \times 3 \times 4 \times 5 \times 6$, which equals 720 different ways. So to figure out the number of ways you could arrange 50 tricks, you would take $1 \times 2 \times 3 \times \ldots \times 50$. This product turns out to be a number so large that it contains 65 digits!

Addition Curiosity

$$1 + 2 = 3$$
$$4 + 5 + 6 = 7 + 8$$
$$9 + 10 + 11 + 12 = 13 + 14 + 15$$
$$16 + 17 + 18 + 19 + 20 = 21 + 22 + 23 + 24$$
etc.

Magic Squares

How would you go about subtracting the squares of two consecutive whole numbers? For example, what does $8^2 - 7^2$ or $20^2 - 19^2$ equal? The trick—simply add the consecutive numbers and you've got the answer. So $8^2 - 7^2 = 8 + 7$, which equals 15. Also, $20^2 - 19^2 = 20 + 19$, which equals 39. Seems almost too good to be true!

Impossible Challenge

When you calculate $1 \div 9$, you get $0.11111\ldots$, when you calculate $2 \div 9$, you get $0.22222\ldots$, and so on. Can you think of two whole numbers that will produce $0.99999\ldots$ when one is divided into the other?   **Answer:** It can't be done, so don't waste your time trying!

Double Your Pleasure

Take any three-digit number and repeat it to form a six-digit number. A number such as 726 would then become 726,726. Now divide the six-digit number by (in any order) 7, 11, and 13. You'll arrive at the original three-digit number every time. For example, $726,726 \div 7 \div 11 \div 13 = 726$. Try it with another three-digit number, and see for yourself!

Triple Your Pleasure

Take any two-digit number and repeat it twice to form a six-digit number. So a number such as 86 would become 868,686. Then divide the six-digit number by (in either order) 91 and 111. You'll arrive at the original two-digit number every time. For example, $868,686 \div 91 \div 111 = 86$. Try it on another two-digit number, and see for yourself!

More Magic Squares

Suppose you'd like to subtract the squares of two numbers, and you'd like to do it quickly. The trick is to add the two numbers, then subtract them, and finally multiply those two amounts together. For example, $7^2 - 4^2 = (7 + 4) \times (7 - 4) = 11 \times 3 = 33$. What about $10^2 - 6^2$? It would equal $(10 + 6) \times (10 - 6) = 16 \times 4 = 64$.

Quick Check

Do you want to know how to quickly check your answer when multiplying by 9, 99, 999, and so forth? Well, there's an amazingly easy way. All you have to do is add up the digits of the product. If that sum can be evenly divided by 9 (that is, if it is 9, 18, 27, etc.), your answer is _probably_ correct. For example, the calculation $99 \times 426 = 42,174$ is probably correct because the digit-sum of the product $(4 + 2 + 1 + 7 + 4)$ is 18. If the sum of the product's digits _cannot_ be divided evenly by 9, then the product is _definitely_ incorrect. So the calculation $64 \times 999 = 63,836$ is definitely incorrect because the product's digit-sum $(6 + 3 + 8 + 3 + 6)$ is 26, which _cannot_ be evenly divided by 9.

The Mysterious Number 9 Revisited

Dividing by 9, 99, 999, and so forth, produces some interesting number patterns. For example, take $2 \div 9$, and you get $0.2222 \ldots$. Take a two-digit number, such as 37, divide by 99, and you get $0.373737 \ldots$. Finally, take a three-digit number, such as 481, divide by 999, and you get $0.481481481 \ldots$. Did you notice the number pattern in each of the answers?

Quick Teaser

Can you figure out a way to quickly add the whole numbers from 1 to n? For example, how would you quickly calculate 1 + 2 + 3 + 4 + 5?

Answer: Take the top number (5, in this case), multiply by the next whole number (6, in this case), and divide the product (30, in this case) by 2 (producing the answer 15, in this case). The formula, therefore, is $\frac{n \times (n + 1)}{2}$, where "n" is the highest number in the series.

The Dangers of Rounding

Rounding is one of the most powerful tools used in the world of rapid calculation. However, one must be extremely careful when determining *to what degree* to round. For example, the circumference of the moon (6,789 miles) is calculated by multiplying its diameter (we'll assume exactly 2,160 miles) by π (3.14159265 . . .). Let's see how inaccurate our calculation would be, given the following rounded values of π:

2,160 × 3	= About 306 miles off
2,160 × 3.1	= About 90 miles off
2,160 × 3.14	= About 3½ miles off
2,160 × 3.142	= About 9/10 of a mile off
2,160 × 3.1416	= About 28 yards off

Mathematical Curiosity 1

142,857 × 1 = 142,857
142,857 × 2 = 285,714 (same digits, different order)
142,857 × 3 = 428,571 (same digits, different order)
142,857 × 4 = 571,428 (same digits, different order)
142,857 × 5 = 714,285 (same digits, different order)
142,857 × 6 = 857,142 (same digits, different order)
142,857 × 7 = 999,999 (here's where the pattern ends!)
(Also note: 142 + 857 = 999, and 14 + 28 + 57 = 99)

Mathematical Curiosity 2

$$111 \div (1 + 1 + 1) = 37$$
$$222 \div (2 + 2 + 2) = 37$$
$$333 \div (3 + 3 + 3) = 37$$
$$444 \div (4 + 4 + 4) = 37$$
$$555 \div (5 + 5 + 5) = 37$$
$$666 \div (6 + 6 + 6) = 37$$
$$777 \div (7 + 7 + 7) = 37$$
$$888 \div (8 + 8 + 8) = 37$$
$$999 \div (9 + 9 + 9) = 37$$

Answers to Exercises

Note: The answers to problem #1 in each section are included in the problem. That's why these start with #2.

TRICK #1

2. 198
3. 233
4. 177
5. 242
6. 280

TRICK #2

2. 95
3. 91
4. 133
5. 102
6. 156

TRICK #3

2. 28
3. 24
4. 30
5. 19
6. 29

TRICK #4

2. 15
3. 17
4. 25
5. 39
6. 47

TRICK #5

2. 18
3. 37
4. 28
5. 46
6. 59

TRICK #6

2. 1,000
3. 5,600
4. 3,300
5. 20,000
6. 18,000

TRICK #7

2. 810
3. 4,600
4. 39
5. 12.3
6. 987

TRICK #8

2. 72
3. 140
4. 108
5. 132
6. 168

TRICK #9

2. 170
3. 130
4. 90
5. 160
6. 240

TRICK #10

2. 792
3. 264
4. 176
5. 627
6. 539

TRICK #11

2. 7,225
3. 4,225
4. 9,025
5. 1,225
6. 5,625

TRICK #12

2. 399
3. 1,224
4. 168
5. 624
6. 9,999

TRICK #13

2. 210
3. 270
4. 390
5. 480
6. 720

TRICK #14

2. 110
3. 108
4. 98
5. 144
6. 288

TRICK #15

2. 38
3. 45
4. 40
5. 52
6. 132

TRICK #16

2. 90
3. 4
4. 17
5. 90
6. 30

TRICK #17

2. 19
3. 28.8
4. 530
5. 74
6. 3.14

TRICK #18

2. 13
3. 24
4. 27
5. 32
6. 45

TRICK #19

2. 3.6
3. 5.4
4. 12.2
5. 9.8
6. 16.8

TRICK #20

2. 4
3. 6
4. 8
5. 5
6. 3

TRICK #21

2. 18
3. 24
4. 28
5. 27
6. 33

TRICK #22

2. 66
3. 82
4. 77
5. 85
6. 97

TRICK #23

2. 79
3. 83
4. 78
5. 81
6. 76

TRICK #24

2. 43
3. 36
4. 22
5. 38
6. 41

TRICK #25

2. 23
3. 56
4. 47
5. 62
6. 49

TRICK #26

2. 8.8
3. 4.2
4. 70
5. 550
6. 1500

TRICK #27

2. 216
3. 117
4. 225
5. 162
6. 234

TRICK #28

2. 252
3. 216
4. 420
5. 204
6. 900

TRICK #29

2. 900
3. 600
4. 1,100
5. 1,400
6. 1,800

TRICK #30

2. 1,681
3. 961
4. 1,521
5. 841
6. 9,801

TRICK #31

2. 3,364
3. 3,025
4. 2,601
5. 3,136
6. 3,481

TRICK #32

2. 120
3. 111
4. 156
5. 126
6. 184

TRICK #33

2. 147
3. 145
4. 234
5. 152
6. 207

TRICK #34

2. 11,124
3. 11,025
4. 11,128
5. 10,812
6. 11,881

TRICK #35

2. 294
3. 930
4. 506
5. 1,272
6. 1,353

TRICK #36

2. 30
3. 15
4. 40
5. 70
6. 50

TRICK #37

2. 4.4
3. 36
4. 3.2
5. 52
6. 16

TRICK #38

2. 25
3. 29
4. 59
5. 27
6. 33

TRICK #39

2. 19
3. 23
4. 49
5. 17
6. 47

TRICK #40

2. 12
3. 17
4. 15.5
5. 14
6. 12.5

TRICK #41

2. 600
   (exact answer = 612)
3. 1,400
   (exact answer = 1,386)
4. 1,300
   (exact answer = 1,326)
5. 2,200
   (exact answer = 2,178)
6. 2,500
   (exact answer = 2,550)

TRICK #42

2. 900
   (exact answer = 918)
3. 2,800
   (exact answer = 2,744)
4. 2,200
   (exact answer = 2,244)
5. 3,600
   (exact answer = 3,528)
6. 4,700
   (exact answer = 4,794)

TRICK #43

2. 1,800
   (exact answer = 1,809)
3. 2,800
   (exact answer = 2,772)
4. 2,600
   (exact answer = 2,613)
5. 5,000
   (exact answer = 4,950)
6. 1,400
   (exact answer = 1,407)

TRICK #44

2. 4.8
   (exact answer is about 4.7)
3. 6.6
   (exact answer = 6.666 . . .)
4. 21
   (exact answer is about 20.6)
5. 7.5
   (exact answer is about 7.58)
6. 9.3
   (exact answer is about 9.1)

TRICK #45

2. 9
   (exact answer is about 8.8)
3. 6.4
   (exact answer is about 6.5)
4. 3.6
   (exact answer is about 3.5)
5. 18.2
   (exact answer is about 18.6)
6. 5.4
   (exact answer is about 5.3)

TRICK #46

2. 12
   (exact answer is about 11.9)
3. 10.5
   (exact answer is about 10.6)
4. 2.7
   (exact answer is about 2.69)
5. 30
   (exact answer is about 30.3)
6. 48
   (exact answer is about 47.8)

TRICK #47

2. 6.82
   (exact answer = 6.888 . . .)
3. 4.4
   (exact answer = 4.444 . . .)
4. 7.7
   (exact answer = 7.777 . . .)
5. 9.35
   (exact answer = 9.444 . . .)
6. 7.59
   (exact answer = 7.666 . . .)

TRICK #48

2. 5.4
   (exact answer is about 5.45)
3. 18
   (exact answer is about 18.2)
4. 63
   (exact answer is about 63.6)
5. 27
   (exact answer is about 27.3)
6. 72
   (exact answer is about 72.7)

TRICK #49

2. Probably correct
3. Probably correct
4. Definitely incorrect
5. Probably correct
6. Definitely incorrect

TRICK #50

2. Definitely incorrect
3. Definitely incorrect
4. Probably correct
5. Probably correct
6. Definitely incorrect